T5-BQA-628

The Sermon in Perspective

The Sermon in Perspective

A STUDY OF COMMUNICATION AND CHARISMA

JAMES EARL MASSEY

BAKER BOOK HOUSE
Grand Rapids, Michigan

To

my teachers

whose conclusions I dared to test

and

my students

who have dared to question mine

PREFACE

Sarah B. Yule recalled a lecture Emerson gave in which he said, "If a man write a better book, preach a better sermon, or make a better mouse-trap than his neighbour, tho' he build his house in the woods, the world will make a beaten path to his door."[1] Even if the returns are not that great, the preacher still owes it to the smaller crowd and to himself to "preach a better sermon," to sharpen his ability to communicate as a spokesman for God.

John Wesley seemed disturbed at one point in his long ministry over what he heard another preacher confess about making better sermons. Wesley remembered the man saying, "Once in seven years I burn all my sermons; for it is a shame if I cannot write better sermons now than I did seven years ago."[2] Wesley demurred at such anxiety, suggesting that his own earlier treatments of certain crucial topics could not be bettered even though his reading had deepened and his knowledge extended. "Whatever others can do," Wesley wrote, "I sadly cannot. I cannot write a better sermon on the Good Steward than I did seven years ago, I cannot write a better on the Great Assize than I did twenty years ago; I cannot write a better on the Use of Money, than I did nearly thirty years ago; nay, I know not that I can write a better on the Circumcision of the Heart than I did five-and-forty years ago. Perhaps, indeed, I may have read five or six hundred books more than I had then,

---

1. *The Oxford Dictionary of Quotations* (New York and London: Oxford University Press, 1956), p. 201.
2. *The Journal of John Wesley*, ed. Percy Livingstone Parker (Chicago: Moody Press, 1952), p. 363.

7

and may know a little more history, or natural philosophy, than I did; but I am not sensible that this has made any essential addition to my knowledge in divinity. Forty years ago I knew and preached every Christian doctrine which I preach now."[3] Wesley made that comment when he was seventy-five years old! How different is George Arthur Buttrick in his eighties, still working away at his sermon preparation, always seeking to exceed his last efforts because "he knows best how close he comes to his own difficult standards."[4]

While there is wisdom in Wesley's refusal to exert himself anxiously beyond conscious dependence upon God's help, yet it must also be stated that the opportunity and obligation to speak demand that we give some priority to planning for improvement. It is wise to involve ourselves in a constant attempt to preach better than before. The reason for preaching demands that we try forever to make our sermons better. This book is addressed to preachers concerned about preaching "a better sermon."

Mention the word *sermon* and certain sensitivities are aroused in both preacher and congregation. Those sensitivities are influenced by some theory or set of experiences—pleasant or unpleasant, and all of these have a direct bearing on how we see the sermon. To the degree that we understand how to view our task, to that degree do we know, understand, and control our approach to that task. Preaching is like every other work: how we see and understand it demands a stance, a place from which to view it, a vantage point from which to perceive and act. Perspective is all-important in making essential assessments and thoughtful planning.

This book discusses the sermon in perspective, from five angles of vision. The sermon is viewed first as communication because it is an act of formal speech with the specific intent to deliver God's message to men. It is viewed next as commentary because sermons are traditionally expected to be an exposition and application of a Biblical text or theme. The sermon is then viewed as counsel because it is backed by a concern to help persons deal with their real needs and life situations. The next chapter deals with "The

3. Ibid.
4. Theodore A. Gill, "Introduction," *To God Be the Glory: Sermons in Honor of George Arthur Buttrick,* ed. Theodore A. Gill (Nashville: Abingdon Press, 1973), p. 8.

Sermon as Creation" and describes the process by which sermons are conceived and shaped for use, while the closing chapter on "The Sermon As Charisma" deals with the *extra* within preaching— personality, projection, feel, thrust, involvement, etc.

All in all, the subject (the sermon) is singular; but the perspective of treatment differs from chapter to chapter. I thought of this while traveling by train from Geneva to Lausanne, Switzerland, last summer. There were several points along the way where Mont Blanc could be seen in the distance, that beautiful peak looming clearly before my eyes every time the position of the train had shifted to give a new vantage point for a fresh and different view. Each chapter of this book shifts our position to help us get a fresh view of the sermon which, properly understood and experienced, is itself a thing of beauty and redemptive benefit.

The basic substance of this book was delivered as the Mary Claire Gautschi Lectures at Fuller Theological Seminary in Pasadena, California, during the Fall Quarter of 1975. The purpose of the lectures is "to bring to the Fuller campus distinguished clergymen who will provide example and encouragement for students preparing for parish ministry." It was a pleasure to be a guest within that community, and I am indebted both to the theological students who responded so warmly to my statements and to the working pastors, many of them long-time friends, who took time out of their very busy schedules to attend and share with the rest of us. The kindnesses of President David A. Hubbard and Dr. Robert N. Schaper during my visit to the campus were exceeded only by my gratitude in being invited to share myself and my thought.

These chapters were also delivered as the 1975 Fall Lectures at Ashland Theological Seminary, Ashland, Ohio. The hospitality accorded me there was characteristic of Dean Joseph R. Schultz and Dr. Louis F. Gough, my long-time friend. I use this occasion to thank them both again.

Some of the chapter sections were used yet again at Gulf-Coast Bible College, Houston, Texas, in February, 1976, during the Fourteenth Annual Ministers' Refresher Institute. I am grateful to President John W. Conley and the institute committee for shaping the program around my choice of topic. The lively interchange following the lectures only deepened my concern to share them with a larger audience.

Thanks are also offered to Mrs. Kathy Freer, who typed the drafts and final copy with alertness, patience, and skill.

JAMES EARL MASSEY

Anderson Graduate School of Theology

CONTENTS

1. The Sermon As . . .

COMMUNICATION

The preaching ministry involves those called to a very comprehensive and challenging endeavor: speaking the Word of God publicly. Crucial to that task is the sermon, a speech form associated almost exclusively with the Gospel and religious insights. The sermon is an ancient channel of communication for sharing God's message to men about the immediates and ultimates of life. Used traditionally in connection with religious or worship occasions, and based upon some text or passage of sacred Scripture, the sermon is quite unlike other speech forms in terms of its motive, setting, spirit, and substance.

Ozora S. Davis, paraphrasing Austin Phelps, has defined a sermon as "an oral message, incorporated into an order of worship, on a religious truth, directed to the popular mind with a view to a decision of the hearers which shall lead them into the Christian experience, individually and socially."[1] This definition is neither full nor final, but it does highlight the major features of the sermon and adequately clarifies those distinctives which mark the sermon as different from other speech and communicative forms.

The designation *sermon* reflects not only a religious purpose but a certain cultural tradition as well. The sermon as we now know it is an adaptation of the Greek rhetorical art form[2] by early Christian leaders intent on communicating the Gospel with speech ef-

---

1. Ozora S. Davis, *Principles of Preaching* (Chicago: The University of Chicago Press, 1924), pp. 184-135. See Austin Phelps, *The Theory of Preaching* (New York: Scribner's, 1899), p. 28.
2. On the history of this speech art, see George Kennedy, *The Art of Persuasion in Greece* (Princeton: Princeton University Press, 1963).

fectiveness. The history and form of the sermon, then, involve us in two fields of inquiry, the broad field of speech culture and the narrower area of Christian proclamation.[3] Interestingly, we do not usually refer to the preacher's speech, but to his sermon. *Speech* is the modern term for *rhetoric*, the older term, and it lacks the rich religious connotations of what we call the sermon or homily. Although we should hold this distinction between a speech and a sermon in mind, we must also recognize a basic relationship and similarity between a speech and a sermon: both are channels of communication, forms of public address, and both are dependent upon methodology and structural forms to help hearers encounter meanings through the use of words.

I

The sermon as we know it is a constant reminder of the influence of speech culture within the Church. As a speech form it is one among the many syngenetic aspects of society on which we are dependent. "A syngenetic element," explains George I. Mavrodes, "is a practice, institution or structure which on the one hand is not automatic, instinctive, or 'natural,' but on the other hand is characteristically not invented or developed by the individual who engages in it. It is something given to us by our fellows and our predecessors, and we take it over and use it."[4] That was the case when the post-Apostolic preachers found ready speech styles and forms which offered striking advantages for handling their communicative concern. In taking over Greek rhetorical forms, these leaders adopted an ancient speech tradition and adapted it for a higher use. It was a natural borrowing on the part of men who were at home in Greek rhetoric and the intellectual culture of the Greco-Roman world. Edwin Hatch thus

---

3. On this area of inquiry, see John Ker, *Lectures on the History of Preaching,* ed. A. R. Macewen (New York: George H. Doran Co., 1889); Hugh Thomson Kerr, *Preaching in the Early Church* (New York: Fleming H. Revell Co., 1942); T. Harwood Pattison, *The History of Christian Preaching* (Philadelphia: American Baptist Publication Society, 1903); Ralph G. Turnbull, *A History of Preaching,* E. C. Dargan Series, vol. III (Grand Rapids: Baker Book House, 1974).
4. George I. Mavrodes, "Christian Philosophy and the Non-Christian Philosopher," *Christian Scholar's Review,* vol. II, no. 4 (1973), p. 327.

asserted that "it [Greek rhetoric] created the Christian sermon."[5] Indeed, "it was natural that when addresses, whether expository or hortatory, came to prevail in the Christian communities, they should be affected by the similar addresses which filled a large place in contemporary Greek life."[6] This overt claiming of that syngenetic element was fortuitous for Christian proclamation. The detailed story of this development shows that the Church Fathers were serious about the business of communication. Sensitive to the Spirit, and committed to Christian truth, those leaders were also sensible about style and they made great exactions upon themselves to be ready communicative agents. They laid hold upon every aid to precondition themselves for sermon effectiveness.

It is lamentable that such diligence is not the common rule among those who preach in our day. While the problem is not peculiar to our day, we do feel the sting from both Church and world as criticisms mount about the lack of ardor and articulateness among those entrusted to speak or preach publicly about God and truth. The problem has to do, in part, with the failure of many preachers to take speech and the communication task with necessary seriousness. Back in 1943, at the very time when a Gallup Poll revealed that 97 percent of the populace considered the sermon as the chief feature in the public worship service, John Nichols Booth was reporting a problem in the Church regarding sermon communication:

> Ministers are nearly alone in the professional world in their unrealistic abhorrence of the basic principles of their speaking art. Musicians analyze the mechanics of style and form; sculptors study anatomy; too many preachers rely on intuition! To learn and and use tested devices developed by past and present authorities in homiletics is to produce better sermons.[7]

But in 1963, twenty years later, the problem was still widespread among the clergy. Kyle Haselden, another concerned observer of preachers and preaching, registered his complaints: "In a day when more people than ever before in the history of language are using public speech with skill and effectiveness, ministers, whose chief tool is the spoken word, have in general less skill and

5. Edwin Hatch, *The Influence of Greek Ideas and Usages upon the Christian Church* (London: Williams and Norgate, 1907), p. 113.

6. Ibid., p. 108.

7. John Nichols Booth, *The Quest for Preaching Power* (New York: The Macmillan Co., 1943), p. xv.

less training in oral communication than men and women in a
host of other professions."[8] Haselden was disturbed by the fact
that "television announcers and commentators show more respect
for the artful possibilities of the human voice than do ministers
who use the same oral capacities for a spiritual rather than a
secular profession."[9]

Since the ministry is now considered as "almost synonymous
with communication,"[10] every preacher needs to review his methods
and efforts for effectiveness as a communicator. Although a full
review would call for examining the many contacts we make and
the complex aspects of the kinds of sharing expected, the need
being stressed here is for a review of the sermon as communication.

II

The sermon is a speech event initiated and given by someone,
to some group, within a given time and place, and for some religious purpose. This "configuration of communication"[11] is both
simple and complex. It is simple in that a long-established speech
pattern is being used, and a long-esteemed tradition is being continued—and with understood purpose. But it is complex in that
certain elemental relations must exist if the speech event is to
achieve its end.

Considering the five elements found in the description just
given—a message, a preacher, a group of listeners, a setting, and a
purpose for the occasion—four sets of relationships are immediately
discerned as involved in the sermon occasion:

1. The Preacher-Sermon Relationship
2. The Sermon-Listener Relationship
3. The Preacher-Listener Relationship
4. The Listener-Setting Relationship.

8. Kyle Haselden, *The Urgency of Preaching* (New York and Evanston: Harper and Row, 1963), p. 21.
9. Ibid.
10. Merrill R. Abbey, *Communication in Pulpit and Parish* (Philadelphia: The
Westminster Press, 1973), p. 15.
11. This designation, used originally in another connection, is that of Paul
I. Rosenthal. See his essay, "The Concept of Ethos and the Structure of Persuasion," *Speech Monographs*, vol. XXXIII, no. 2 (June 1966), pp. 120-121.

Please observe that one element appears in three of the four relationships mentioned, namely the listener. These relationships involving preacher, sermon, listener, and setting must be considered with seriousness because they remind us that communication is a dynamic process, and there is the need always to keep the personal element in the process in clear view. Although the purpose of the sermon provides the controlling element, the personal level of the sharing will be strategic and imperative. The delivery and the hearing of a sermon demand a dynamic process between preacher and listener. The meanings and purpose of a sermon demand a personal level of appeal and appropriate interaction.

Some of the insights from modern communication theory and research can help us to plan for and achieve such results. Here are three guiding principles based on some of those insights.

1. Communication is aided when we *approach the listener at his hearing level*. This hearing level of which I speak does not involve the volume of sound from the preacher but rather involves the listener's system of values; it is not related to the pitch of the preacher's voice but rather to the perception of the listener. Since communication is a process, achieving the sermon purpose depends greatly upon what is perceived in relation to what is being said. Hearing level has to do with who, what, and where the listener is: his attitudes, beliefs, and experience; his interests, needs, and emotional make-up; his ideas, hopes, environment, and personal hunger. The listener hears in relation to the influence of all these factors upon his perception. As Raymond S. Ross summarily states it, "Listening is much more than hearing acuity."[12]

The influence of these factors upon a listener's hearing situation has prompted needed research and writing about a "psychology for preaching."[13] As in all other communication settings, preaching is also subject to the psychology of thought influencing the way we listen and perceive. Personality theorists have insisted rightly that "purposes, aims, and intentions suffuse the very act

12. Raymond S. Ross, *Speech Communication: Fundamentals and Practice* (Englewood Cliffs: Prentice-Hall, Inc., 1965), p. 8. See also Ross's more extended discussion about hearing on pp. 8-19.
13. See Edgar N. Jackson, *A Psychology for Preaching* (Great Neck, N.Y.: Channel Press, Inc., 1961). See also Clement Welsh, *Preaching in A New Key: Studies in the Psychology of Thinking and Listening* (Philadelphia: Pilgrim Press, 1974).

of perceiving."[14] A listener's reactions, choices, and actions relate most acutely to the extent his doors of perception stand open. The listener is a perceiving person with states of mind which must be acknowledged, understood, respected as personal, and as worthy of being engaged. The sermon is more likely to be heard when the listener is granted such regard and is made to sense the preacher's openness to him as a person. The listener has spent his life—however long or short—perceiving and processing informational elements which have come to him in his life setting. His perception has made him self-aware and life-aware. The sermon must be designed to make him God-aware, with an understanding of the implications which follow from that awareness for his total experience. Preaching was ordained to help men "become like God," affirmed Chrysostom, "in such wise as men might become so."[15] With this end in view the preacher must possess the skill to anticipate and discover the listener's hearing level, and work with understanding and words to widen the doors of his perception for needed engagement with God.

2. Communication through the sermon is aided when we *encourage the hearer's participation*. Any good sermon is developed with a basic design to gain and maintain the listener's interest, and encourage him to be actively present. That sermon design will certainly involve a theme or topic that holds promise, an introduction that excites interest to pursue it, a treatment that releases information and meaning in strategic sequence, proportion, and timeliness, together with an application of that meaning that stirs the listener to a positive and whole response.

The participation we seek must involve the listener's mind and heart. In our attempt to engage the listener, we must anticipate agreement or disagreement, hesitancy or bold response, suspended judgment or ready decision; we must be prepared for selfish resistance, a look of critical questioning, and, in some instances, unquestioning acceptance. In all of these possible responses, the listener is influenced by his dignity and his frailty,

14. George S. Klein, *Perception, Motives and Personality* (New York: Alfred A. Knopf, 1970), p. 129; Klein's study traces the interplay between motives and perception, and explores the basis for a personality theory of perception; see esp. pp. 30-114, 129-161.
15. See his sermon on Matthew 18:4, in *Homilies on the Gospel of Saint Matthew*.

by what holds promise and is pleasing as over against that which challenges, smacks of risk, poses a threat, or makes demand for some change. Our eagerness to engage the listener to be actively present must be matched by anticipation of how he might react. We must be alert to active feedback from the listener: his facial expressions can suggest his reasoned agreement, reflective approval, joyful awareness of a new insight or fact, calm acceptance of some argument, surprise over some statement; or they can show the uneasiness of indecision, tenseness under the pressure of a challenge, deepened self-consciousness through a look of shame, or a sense of pleasure over having some notion confirmed or choice commended.

Encouraging full participation by the listener is not always an easy matter. Many factors will influence the ease or difficulty of the hearing situation. First on the list is his state of mind. The place and setting are also involved. Or consider the subject matter of the sermon, or even the preacher's approach and style. Where a hearing difficulty is anticipated the preacher must act with readiness and build a bridge across the gulf he discovers between himself and the hearer. This is especially the case when the purpose of the sermon is to persuade the listener to embrace some view, make some change, enlist in some cause, promote some concern, dare some deed, or fulfill some responsibility.

An excellent example of this is found in Harry Emerson Fosdick's sermon "Stand By the Church." The sermon was preached on a Budget Sunday during his lengthy and historic pastorate at the Riverside Church in New York. Using a sermon title which clearly voiced an appeal, Fosdick began in earnest, admitting his intentions while anticipating the usual human bias against financial appeals. Fosdick announced:

> This is Budget Sunday, the one occasion in the year when we present to our congregation the financial needs of the parish. Neither to the preacher nor to the congregation is the prospect of a sermon on finance especially alluring. Nevertheless, give me a fair chance to point out how surely financial responsibility is involved in a sincere Christian life.[16]

Then, with a touch of thoughtful humor to soften initial reluc-

---

16. Harry Emerson Fosdick, "Stand By the Church," *Successful Fund-Raising Sermons,* ed. Julius King (New York: Funk and Wagnalls Co., 1953), p. 43.

tance or resistance, Fosdick surprised the hearers with a brief story strategic for giving him immediate psychological control.

> Once Dr. John Hutton, the English preacher, went to his pulpit and as he was giving out his text saw one member of his congregation settling down comfortably for a snooze. Said Dr. Hutton: "If anyone can fall asleep while I am preaching, he is fully entitled so to do; the blame is mine. But a friend here today is taking an unfair advantage of me. He is going to sleep before I get going. No! No! We must start fair!" I make that bargain with you on Budget Sunday.[17]

The illustration did more than interest the listeners, it disarmed criticism. The preacher's approach was factual, blended with a bit of interesting humor. Fosdick stated his claim with forthrightness, and, lifting to view the Christian responsibility to support the work of the Church as God's agent in the world, he made a plain appeal to his motive, right from the start. His audience and subject matter demanded this strategic and disarming start.

He sustained interest by a well-planned sermon design setting forth four bases to illustrate the validity of the Church's claim upon the listener for monetary support. Using apt illustrations for each step in his four point argument, with strong statements of challenge interspersed, Fosdick pressed the issue upon the hearers' minds and hearts, and the reasons behind his claim tightened the circle until each listener felt that claim in a very personal way. Fosdick's sermon was planned and delivered to inform the listeners about their duty and to arouse their hearts to fulfill that duty.

Blaise Pascal (1623-1662) had much to say about involving mind and heart in his brief but pointed essay on "The Art of Persuasion."[18] Pascal underscored the use of verbal precision (facts) and "suggestive feeling" (pleasing appeal) as important in arousing men to understanding, belief, and responsible actions in faith. Pascal had insight into men: how to discover openings in men, bring them to readiness for hearing, remain sensitive to what must be said to them, and communicate to them with naturalness and convincing abandon.

The sermon as communication stands fulfilled in an informed,

17. Ibid.
18. See *Great Shorter Works of Pascal,* trans. Emile Cailliet and John C. Blankenagel (Philadelphia: The Westminster Press, 1948), esp. p. 202. See also Roger Hazelton, *Blaise Pascal: The Genius of His Thought* (Philadelphia: The Westminster Press, 1974), esp. pp. 146-175.

aroused, and God-committed person. Pascal stressed the wedding of facts and engendered feeling in achieving this result. Honest about deep-seated sinfulness and faulty human reactions, Pascal knew that we must disturb a man's complacency before we can bring him to a state of concern; a man's will must be assaulted through truth spoken forcefully to his heart. "It is the heart that feels God, and not reason. That is what faith is: God felt by the heart, not by the reason."[19] The arousal of the heart was crucial in Pascal's exposition of Christian communication.

This imperative of inward arousal is also stressed by Soren Kierkegaard (1813-1855). In his discussions on communication theory, Kierkegaard moved well beyond considerations of logic, structure, aesthetics, and speech setting and highlighted subjectivity as essential to the reception of truth.[20] By subjectivity he meant the sense of relation between the person's whole being and what is said.[21] Again this reminds us that the level and design of a sermon must take into account the listener's consciousness of himself and his experiences. It is to a listener's inward domain that we preach, and the boundaries of that domain influence his perception, understanding, feelings, choices, and actions. We prepare and preach to enter into that inward domain and arouse the hearer to a whole response to God.

Kierkegaard discussed the listener's need for clarity of mind about what he is to do, and stated that clarity results from truth which yields the "understanding [which] must precede every action."[22] Speaking personally, Kierkegaard went on to say, "The thing is to understand myself, to see what God really wishes *me* to do; the thing is to find which is *for me*, to find *the idea for*

19. *Pensée* 627, in *Pascal's Pensées*, Bi-Lingual Edition with Translation, Notes and Introduction by H. F. Stewart (New York: Pantheon Books, 1950). This rendering is from the French (p. 344) and differs slightly in style from Stewart's translation on p. 345.
20. On Kierkegaard's rhetorical theory, see Raymond E. Anderson, "Kierkegaard's Theory of Communication," *Speech Monographs*, vol. XXX, no. 1 (March 1963), pp. 1-14; Gregor Malantschuk, *Kierkegaard's Way to the Truth*, trans. Mary Michelsen (Minneapolis: Augsburg Publishing House, 1963), esp. pp. 114-119; Herman Diem, *Kierkegaard: An Introduction*, trans. David Green (Richmond: John Knox Press, 1966), esp. pp. 19-28.
21. See Edward John Carnell, *The Burden of Soren Kierkegaard* (Grand Rapids: William B. Eerdmans Publishing Co., 1965), esp. pp. 56-89, 124-164.
22. *The Journals of Soren Kierkegaard: A Selection Edited and Translated by Alexander Dru* (London: Oxford University Press, 1938), p. 15.

which I can live and die."[23] The sermon communicates properly when each listener hears that which grants an "imperative of understanding"[24] and arouses him to receive fully what is spoken into his life. This result is the preacher's aim. We preach sermons to communicate, moving listeners from a sense of possibility (thought constructs) to a sense of necessity (heart-life arousal), out of which issues the decision to make commitment actual.

Much of what is being said here reflects the concern to persuade. This, I affirm, is a basic end in preaching. In Christian proclamation the need to persuade men is quite primary; stimulation, belief, and action usually grow out of this key result. Addressing ourselves to the hearer, appealing to his "interiority," freedom, and sense of alternatives, our sermonic effort to communicate will largely involve the need and ability to be persuasive.

3. As communicative process, the sermon demands more than giving worded reality: it calls for *the honest giving of a self*. Sermons are "made or broken" by the personal flavor of the spokesman: his spirit, attitudes, character.

Dr. Joseph Parker, noted English preacher, ran an Institute of Homiletics even while he pastored. Many ministers and theological students attended during the three years of the life of that school and were helped by Parker's teaching and insights. One young preacher attended who had never been able to secure a pastorate for himself; he sought Parker's advice as to where his deficiency lay. The considerate teacher had the young man preach for him, addressing him as he would a congregation. The sermon completed, Parker advised:

> I will tell you exactly the conclusion I have come to on hearing your sermon. Throughout it all you spoke as if you were more anxious to get something off *your* mind than to get something into *mine*. That must be fatal to any ministry, which should not be to relieve the preacher's memory of a burden, but to edify his hearers by imparting to them the truth.[25]

The young would-be pastor would have to learn how to give himself as well as his statement.

Long, long ago, in one of the earliest, most ably written, and

23. Ibid.
24. Ibid.
25. William Adamson, *The Life of Joseph Parker* (New York: Fleming H. Revell Co., 1902), p. 92.

wisest treatments of the speaking art, Aristotle commented on this personal aspect of public speaking. "As for the speakers themselves," he wrote, "the sources of our trust in them are three, for apart from the arguments there are three things that gain our belief, namely, intelligence, character, and good will."[26] Aristotle was discussing the *ethos*, or ethics, of persuasion. A speaker who shows intelligence prompts our trust that he will not express wrong opinions. If he has character, this offsets mistrust of his motives, while a sense of good will generated by the speaker assures the hearer that he is respected and not being manipulated. Aristotle added, "It necessarily follows that the speaker who is thought to have all these qualities has the confidence of his hearers."[27]

The importance of *ethos* in Christian preaching is obvious. The nature and purpose of the sermon requires both credibility and a favorable audience perception. The personal qualities of the preacher are crucial to such belief and acceptance. An important question with which the preacher must wrestle as he delivers his sermon is this: In what light am I being seen and perceived?[28]

The working pastor usually has an advantage in this respect over any others who come in to deliver sermons as guest preachers to his congregation. The pastor is seen and perceived in light of both his relations and responsibility. He is a known figure, and if his behavior and work have matched the members' needs and expectations, then all benefits from their personal trust and regard accrue to his credit when he stands to preach to them. The pastor's role as ordained servant in the Church helps to encourage credibility, while his apt handling of opportunities and duties helps to deepen it. The dynamics of a sermon involve more than a strong

---

26. Aristotle, *Rhetoric,* trans. Lane Cooper (New York: Appleton-Century-Crofts, Inc., 1932), pp. 91-92.
27. Ibid., p. 92.
28. The answer to this question is given in large part by feedback. For suggestive discussion about audience perception tests, see Gerald R. Miller, "Speech: An Approach to Human Communication," *Approaches to Human Communication,* ed. Richard W. Budd and Brent D. Ruben (New York and Washington: Spartan Books, 1972), esp. pp. 385-388, and selected sources listed among his references (pp. 398-400). Merrill R. Abbey's *Communication in Pulpit and Parish* (Philadelphia: The Westminster Press, 1973) discusses preaching in the light of the new insights from communication research and offers strategic guidance on the fundamentals of speech and fresh innovations for sermon effectiveness. For Abbey's treatment of the feedback factor, see esp. pp. 44, 47-51, 53-54, 91-94.

idea or insight whose time has come. The preacher's character must encourage trust and a sense of openness. Christian communication calls for more than vocal doing, it requires a certain kind and style of being. The sermon as communication is aided by expressive style, but its effectiveness is all the more assured by the spokesman's character and spirit.

Michelangelo (1475-1564) loved to hear Savonarola preach. The younger man's life and art fell under that reformer's spell. Although sometimes extravagant in speech and extreme in approach, Savonarola well knew his mission of preaching, and he set out to conquer the hearts and wills of men for God. Wedding the rules of speech to the simplicity of sound doctrine, that preacher performed his preaching task with all the sincerity, Biblical understanding, conviction, natural emotion, spontaneity, and concern that his life made available. His honesty and tremendous earnestness made him attractive and acceptable despite his eccentricities. Michelangelo was only one of many attracted and blessed by that reformer's life and work. One of the biographers of Savonarola reported, "We know that Michelangelo carried to his tomb the remembrance of Fra Hieronymo deeply graven on his heart, and Michelangelo survived him nearly seventy years.[29] It is no wonder that the artist considered his own work of painting and sculpting as religious creations, as "sermons-in-pigment," and his art as a handmaid to theology.[30] There was more at work in his lofty view of art than mere respect for and loyalty to the prevailing Church order. A tested, trusted preacher had impressed him, a preacher whose sermons had achieved emotional communion with his audience. "The devotion he aroused in his followers, of every type and class, was the best tribute to a charm and attraction which perhaps today is not very easy to understand,"[31] except for those who too have known the attractive power of some preacher's charismatic *ethos*.[32]

The longer I preach, and the more experience I gather as I

29. E. L. S. Horsburgh, *Girolamo Savonarola* (London: Methuen and Co., Ltd., 1911), p. 96.
30. See Robert J. Clements, *Michelangelo's Theory of Art* (London: Routledge and Kegan Paul, 1963), esp. pp. 72-73.
31. Michael de la Bedoyere, *The Meddlesome Friar: The Story of the Conflict Between Savonarola and Alexander VI* (London: Collins, 1958), p. 159.
32. See the author's more extended treatment of this factor in ch. 5 of this book.

preach, the deeper grows my conviction that what people want from and through a sermon is true *soul*, which is but a more contemporary, brief (and ethnic) word for what Phillips Brooks stressed when he told the Yale Divinity School audience that "preaching is the bringing of truth through personality."[33] "It has in it two essential elements, truth and personality. Neither of those can it spare and still be preaching," said Brooks.[34]

We are called to make the hearing occasion an historic occasion. Our listeners are not blessed by mere faultless flow of speech, by progressive handling of well-ordered learning, by the most adroit plan to engage them at the level of emotion nor by a high sense of suggestiveness. Preaching makes the hearing occasion historic when the heart of the preacher is shared with the hearer, blending the preacher's wisdom and warmth, logic and love, statement and self with the hearer's presence. This kind of experience *is* historic; and it has a continuing ministry in memory and in life. When the sermon truly communicates, history is made. This is the case whether the preacher speaks in stately style, quite straightforward and businesslike in his thrust, moving through his designed approach with cool efficiency, or whether by passionate statement, endearing gestures, and overt enthusiasm he heightens the hearer's emotional level of awareness. If we give our heart as we speak our word, the truth is served, and personality is both released and touched, making communication real. Savonarola is credited with achieving "emotional communion with his audience."[35] Savonarola was a true soul preacher.

III

And now a word about the sermon setting. The sermon is delivered and heard, more often than not, during a service of worship. It therefore partakes of ritual as part of a wider context of activity in celebration of God. As one of the preacher's major responsibilities during the experience of group worship, the sermon

---

33. Phillips Brooks, *Lectures on Preaching* (New York: E. P. Dutton and Co., 1907), p. 5.
34. Ibid.
35. Ralph Roeder, *Savonarola: A Study in Conscience* (New York: Brentano's Publishers, 1930), p. 51.

is his formal contribution in speech within a pattern of activity whose range of dynamics can be most determinative in shaping views, values, and behavior. We are accustomed to discussions about the content and thrust of sermons as delivered, but we should not overlook the ritual setting of that delivery.

As communication, the sermon is affected by the setting within which it is preached, by its place within the sequence of worship activities, by the relationship between its own theme design and the theme and order of the service. As communication, the sermon is also affected by its correspondence as speech product with the religious speech culture of the worshiping group.

Given our tradition as organized churches, and given the place of the sermon in group worship, we must not overlook the bearing this ritual setting has on the hearing occasion. Fixed rites and forms influence perception, expectation, and degrees of involvement. The whole pattern of the usual worship ceremony involves a traditional time for gathering, a special place (church sanctuary) with special materials as aids to worship (Sunday bulletin, Bible, hymnal), authorized persons to guide the experience (ministers, choir), special forms of language in connection with certain actions (prayers: the pastoral prayer, offertory, dedication, benediction), and an understood purpose that presides over the entire time together—the celebration of God. If the setting is adequately organized and controlled, so that cultural factors are not a limiting secularity, even the ritual can be revelational and a means of touching the soul. Where ritual might sometimes fail to effect this, however, the sermon is still expected to succeed.

The expectations of church members regarding sermons should be considered as a plus element in the worship service, and as a vote of confidence in the preacher as God's spokesman. Although many of these expectations are quite culturally conditioned, certain dynamics are at work in them to make the members present, alert, and expectant, and thus to grant the preacher opportunity to share his word on a still deeper level of need. When he has concerned himself to pray about the members and to trace out the implications of his word for their lives; when he has been pushed to his pulpit by a desire and commitment to share with them his message and his anointed mission; and when he has prepared himself and his truths to be heard, the hungry will look up, being fed, and the ailing will find healing and strength. Godly expectations are not left unmet when the sermon is preached as the preacher's act of worship, personal in its thrust to meet identifiable needs and concerns, and when, rooted in the insights of the Word of God, it is delivered with a sense of partnership with God.[36]

I have spoken of godly expectations. There are some other expectations to which sermons can be addressed. In dealing with certain expectations of his people about preaching, the preacher must avoid some obvious dangers, the chief of which is to cater to their whims, emotional concerns, or pleasure. As for pleasing men, that temptation can take many forms and must therefore be watched on all levels. Interestingly, the preacher's speech culture and sermon style can fall into this trap.

St. John Chrysostom (354?-407) tried hard to avoid this pitfall as he preached. When he became aware that his rhetorical competence was at times a stumbling block to his true message, Chrysostom lamented the problem posed by speech artistry. He found that public expectations for elaborate phraseology can lead to vanity and evil affectations. When some of his hearers delighted in his style and missed the essential content of his sermons, he rebuked them. The tone and strength of the rebuke are quite clear in this passage from one of his sermons in a series on the Acts of the Apostles:

> Believe me, I speak not other than I feel—when as I discourse I hear myself applauded, at the moment indeed I feel it as a man (for why should I not own the truth?): I am delighted, and give way to the pleasurable feeling: but when I get home, and bethink me that those who applauded received no benefit from my discourse, but that whatever benefit they ought to have got, they lost it while applauding and praising, I am in pain, and groan, and weep, and feel as if I had spoken all in vain. I say to myself: "What profit comes to me from my labors, while the hearers do not choose to benefit by what they hear from us?" Nay, often have I thought to make a rule which should prevent all applauding, and persuade you to listen with silence and becoming orderliness. But bear with me, I beseech you, and be persuaded by me, and, if it seem good to you, let us even now establish this rule, that no hearer be permitted to applaud in the midst of any person's discourse, but if he will needs admire, let him admire in silence: there

---

36. On this, see my book *The Responsible Pulpit* (Anderson, Ind.: The Warner Press, 1974), esp. pp. 79-85.

> is none to prevent him: and let all his study and eager desire
> be set upon the receiving the things spoken.[37]

Chrysostom was trying to stop his members from following the
custom, common in the public theaters, of showing approbation
to a speaker through applause. The pastor's regulation was suggested to keep the religious setting under proper control as an atmosphere for hearing and regard before God. He wanted to keep
expectations centered upon meaning and commitment rather than
upon pleasurable excursions into emotional heights through rhetoric
and word-consciousness. Chrysostom offered a strategic challenge:
"So shall we lay the whole stress of our time and diligence not
upon arts of composition and beauties of expression, but upon
the matter and meaning of the thoughts."[38]

The unwary might be tempted to equate such applause with
acceptance of the "matter and meaning of the [preacher's] thoughts."
But Chrysostom knew better. He wanted to see that meaning
lived by his hearers, and he wanted to rid the worship setting of
such antics and human acclaim for the speaker. Some would see
audience display as but proof of the hearer's involvement, a ready
indication that he has been fully engaged as participant. But not
all agreement is understanding, and not every "amen" is being
said to God. This has been brought forcibly to my attention from
several years of service among audiences within the Black Church
tradition, as it is called. In that tradition, which shaped and nour-
ished my life, arousal is the result expected from a worship service,
and especially from a sermon. Now, arousal must involve mind
and heart, as Pascal insisted, but it can also involve hands and
feet! Given the Black Church tradition of festive sermons and the
dynamic communalism of pastor-people responses during worship,[39]
the levels of engagement and sharing are multiple indeed. With a
sermon tradition that is itself a rhetorical art form—highlighting
rhythmic cadences, memorable sentences, catchy phrases, striking

---

37. Chrysostom, Homily XXX, Acts XIII.42, *Nicene and Post-Nicene Fathers
of the Christian Church*, ed. Philip Schaff (Grand Rapids: William B. Eerdmans Publishing Co., 1956), vol. XI, p. 193. For an excellent study of Chrysostom's rhetorical skill in preaching, see *The Preaching of Chrysostom*, ed. Jero-
slav Pelikan, The Preacher's Paperback Library (Philadelphia: Fortress Press,
1967), esp. 19-28; Donald Attwater, *St. John Chrysostom: Pastor and Preacher*
(London: Harvill Press, 1959).
38. Chrysostom, Homily XXX, *Fathers*, ed. Schaff, p. 194.
39. See Massey, *The Responsible Pulpit*, esp. 102-105.

aphorisms, unrestrained speech, "tonal variations that energize, envelop, and stir the worshipers to share their faith even emotionally,"[40] the proclivity to audible response by the church has at times been problematic—and worthy of the criticism voiced by Chrysostom against applauding for the wrong reasons. It is possible, in such a free setting, to listen without hearing, and to enjoy without being redemptively engaged. In any setting where cultural factors are readily at work and the actions that occur are "symbolically important,"[41] the preacher must be watchful and guard the hearers against stopping short of *lived* truth.

I grew up in a church tradition where some measure of verbal response was allowed and expected from the listening congregation. I have on occasion watched the responses of preachers who did not have this in their background, and who work regularly in a context where such is not the custom. Upon hearing an "Amen," some of those I watched registered mild shock, which became glad surprise, and, finally, impetus to repeat the word. I have also cringed in sympathy while some preachers lost their train of thought under the unexpected assault of some worshiper's ejaculatory prayer— "Lord, help him!" It is not always easy for leaders unaccustomed to this audience freedom to interpret properly the meaning of what is said. In some cases, the pastor must later help the audience to understand, or confirm for them what opened up psychologically as the sermon progressed.

Preacher Stephen T. Szilagyi, a native of Czechoslovakia, and a 1952 immigrant to the United States, told of his reaction to this free church response as he was preaching. "On one occasion I delivered a message in a church, when all of a sudden, someone in the congregation said 'Amen.' It shocked me. But realizing that he was agreeing with me, I repeated the same sentence over again, and he came back with another 'Amen,' and two more joined him. Soon I was getting these 'Amens' left and right. After I got through, the minister from the church said to me, 'Your sermon rated very high. You received about twenty-four "Amens." This is an excellent

40. Ibid., pp. 104-105.
41. See Henry H. Mitchell, "Black Preaching," *The Black Christian Experience,* comp. Emmanuel L. McCall (Nashville: Broadman Press, 1972), p. 57; see also Mitchell's more extensive treatment on this in *Black Preaching* (Philadelphia: J. B. Lippincott Co., 1970), esp. chs. VII-VIII.

rating for a sermon.' "[42] There are times when this is so, thank
God. But there are also times when the "Amens" and personal
responses are but habits from cultural conditioning and should not
be mistaken as honest signs of consent, attitude change, or spiritual
commitment. The dynamics of a setting must be understood for
what they are, and they must be harnessed in the interest of what
they should help to do.

IV

As communication, the sermon is best understood, then, as a
way of sharing with men "a word from the Lord." A truly Christian sermon serves the interests of divine revelation. This is what
Karl Barth sought to underscore when he wrote, "Not general
reflections on man and the cosmos but Revelation is the only le-
gitimate ground for preaching."[43]

The Christian sermon holds a major relation with the *kerygma,*
and it promotes the content and implications of the *kerygma* for
faith, hope, and nurture. This particularity within the Christian
sermon is religious, but it is more: it carries us beyond religious
tradition, popular ethics, and humanitarian concerns to the key
message of the faith. It goes beyond a statement of values to an
interpretation of Jesus as the revealed Son of God and Saving
Person. The Christian sermon maintains its integrity only as it
honors its *raison d'être.* It should stand in the apostolic tradition
and that tradition must influence it logically, theologically, and
actually. The Christian sermon majors in presenting particularized
truth—"the truth [that] is in Jesus" (Eph. 4:21), truth through *His*
personality, truth offered to make and sustain men as new crea-
tures in Christ. Thus Hugh Thomson Kerr has written: "The New
Testament is and always will be our best textbook on preaching.
. . . It presents not only the best technique of preaching but the
only message that justifies the name of preaching."[44]

We have reminded ourselves about the background of the

42. *White House Sermons,* ed. Ben Hibbs (New York and Evanston: Harper
and Row, 1972), pp. 173-174.
43. Karl Barth, *The Preaching of the Gospel,* trans. B. E. Hooke (Philadelphia:
The Westminster Press, 1963), p. 22.
44. Hugh Thomson Kerr, *Preaching in the Early Church* (New York: Fleming
H. Revell Co., 1942), p. 13.

Christian sermon, and have seen how sermon structure and style have been influenced by cultural and rhetorical elements related to human discourse as an art. But we have also reminded ourselves that the spirit and impetus of the sermon are influenced not by culture but by Christ. A worthy sermon stands rooted, then, in Christ while it follows faithfully the canons of communication. As a speech event, the sermon receives from both Christ and the culture. The dynamics at work in preparing and preaching a sermon are multiple. Those dynamics involve reason as well as revelation, psychological effect as well as spiritual inspiration, social perspective as well as "the communication of the Spirit," modality as well as "anointing," and group expectation as well as the message. It might well be said that cultural factors in the sermon are almost consubstantial with its spiritual purpose.

I have called attention earlier to some of the master preachers who were men with acknowledged affinities for speech culture. This takes nothing from their preaching, it rather serves to clarify our understanding of how the revelational factor and the cultural factors relate. It also shows how the commitment of such men to be preachers carried them beyond the limited concerns of rhetoric. The background of the sermon is revelation. The content of the sermon is revelation. The purpose of the sermon is revelation: revelation spoken to confess faith, elicit faith, sustain and direct faith.

In recent years an increased concern has developed to shape what might be called a theology of communication.[45] The interested observer can note with appreciation the balance that the best materials written on this matter strike between what is theology and what is communication art. As the preacher keeps both in mind, his work as spokesman is enhanced.

Lynn Harold Hough, speaking about the Christian pulpit, commented:

> It is here that the Christian criticism of life will most fully and
> decisively and characteristically express itself. And so, we dare

---

45. See Henrik Kraemer, *The Communication of the Christian Faith* (Philadelphia: The Westminster Press, 1956); Eugene A. Nida, *Message and Mission: The Communication of the Christian Faith* (New York: Harper and Row, 1960); Martin Marty, *The Improper Opinion* (Philadelphia: The Westminster Press, 1961), esp. pp. 67-85. J. Harold Ellens, "A Theology of Communication: Putting the Question," *Journal of Psychology and Theology*, vol. II, no. 2 (Spring 1974), pp. 132-139.

believe, will come that renaissance of preaching which will not only bring new power to the church, but which will also bring new life to the world. . . . We have heard all the falsehoods. We have heard all the voices of brilliant confusion. We have heard all the half-truths which betray truth itself. Now the time has come to hear once more with the new vitality of its relation to this new age the great historic voice which sees the human problem in the terms of the Christian solution, and which utters with complete assurance the imperial message of the Christian religion.[46]

Hendrik Kraemer echoes Hough's words about the "imperial message" of our faith, reminding us about "the imperious character" of our work as Christian preachers.[47] The power of the Christian sermon finds its richest explanation in such vivid descriptions as these.

V

Kathleen Neill Nyberg, perceptive writer and wife of a working pastor, commented in one of her books that "The continued acceptance of the sermon in our culture is something of a phenomenon. When we consider the constant barrage of written and spoken words endured by modern man, one wonders with surprise about the large number of people who submit themselves Sunday after Sunday to the words of a preacher. . . . The people enjoy much prerogative in the matter of what they will and will not hear. The sermon deserves to be taken seriously, therefore, and ought to ɩeceive first-class attention and labor."[48] Kathleen Nyberg was writing to other ministers' wives, emphasizing her respect for those periods in her husband's life when he needs undistracted time for work on his sermons.

The sermon does deserve to be taken seriously, and it should receive first-class attention and labor. Sermon work does demand time—and proper tools, together with deep intent on the preacher's part. At a time when, as Mrs. Nyberg mentions, people are exer-

---

46. Lynn Harold Hough, *The Christian Criticism of Life* (Nashville: Abingdon-Cokesbury Press, 1941), pp. 301-302.

47. Kraemer, *Communication*, p. 14.

48. Kathleen Neill Nyberg, *The Care and Feeding of Ministers* (Nashville: Abingdon Press, 1961), p. 104.

cising "much prerogative in the matter of what they will and will not hear," whether they will come or stay away, we must make sure that any decline in attendance at our preaching services is not due to a lack of "first-class attention and labor" on our part. Dr. David H. C. Read remarked in his latest book about a discouraged preacher and friend of his who spoke ruefully to him that Paul ought to have written "How shall [preachers] preach without a hearer?"[49] In discouragement we hardly view the empty pew as a call to prepare and preach a better sermon—and yet it can be such a call! Many factors can work together and cause a church to shrink; in many churches poor preaching is one of those factors. It is time for us to give "first-class attention and labor" with respect to the sermon as communication.

It is time to revitalize our sermons: time to increase our verbal and vocal skill, matching language, thought, voice, and heart to speak "a word from the Lord" with effectiveness. An intensive review of learning theory can help us to take the listening levels of our hearers into account so that we will be heard. As Paul put it, "So faith comes from what is heard...." (Rom. 10:17a). Our regard to shape the occasion for interaction aids that hearing process, helping us to involve the listener as a participant. It is time to shape our statements with anticipation of men's questions, concerns, and needs, appealing with concern to their heart-life. It is time for our sermons to bear the forceful attraction of character, Biblical truth, well-processed thought, and "soul." All of these elements must be at work if we would give better sermons and achieve effective communication. It is time again to blend art with purpose, drama with doctrine, creative approach with basic commentary. Although we realize all the while that in preaching art can be a danger if not kept subordinated to purpose, we also know that purpose can be void of appeal when it lacks artful handling. Our sermons should and can be more effective agencies for communication.

A sermon is an "imperial message." It is a spoken means to help a hearer undergo an experience of religious importance. Our language, content, and style all relate most directly to this end. As for undergoing an experience, Martin Heidegger has explained:

---

49. David H. C. Read, *Sent From God: The Enduring Power and Mystery of Preaching* (Nashville: Abingdon Press, 1974), p. 15.

> To undergo an experience with something—be it a thing, a person, or a god—means that this something befalls us, strikes us, comes over us, overwhelms and transforms us. When we talk of "undergoing" an experience, we mean specifically that the experience is not of our own making; to undergo here means that we endure it, suffer it, receive it as it strikes us and submit to it. It is this something itself that comes about, comes to pass, happens.[50]

The sermon is a prelude to what can come about and happen: encounter, faith, hope, forgiveness, peace of mind and soul, love, direction, understanding, commitment, nurture, service, sustenance, readiness for life and death. The vivid, lively, and unpretentious handling of the Word can put life in perspective for the hearer and grant essential direction for living. Hearing "a word from the Lord" in direct address through the speaking agent can set the self free: free to be and become, free to do and serve, free to respond and share. It is a freedom *from* and a freedom *to:* freedom from doubts, fears, fantasies, and freedom to full participation in the drama of saving grace. The sermon that serves the truth of the Gospel helps to effect these grand and needed results. The nature and importance of this communicative task demands the best we can give in readying ourselves to fulfill it.

Diagram No. 1
PREACHING AND THE LISTENING PROCESS
The Occasion of Hearing

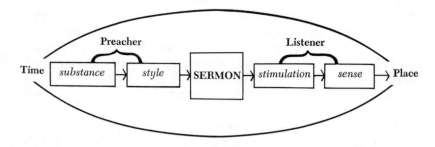

* Adapted from a model by Claude Shannon (1948). See Alfred G. Smith, reflecting Claude Shannon, *Communication and Culture* (New York: Holt, Rinehart and Winston, 1966), p. 17.

50. Martin Heidegger, *On the Way to Language,* trans. Peter D. Hertz (New York and Evanston: Harper and Row, 1971), p. 57.

2. The Sermon As . . .

COMMENTARY

Considered historically, the sermon has usually been a commentary on Scriptural materials and meanings, all for the sake of faith, hope, behavior, and learning. The sermon has been a means for restating, reciting, interpreting, and applying the Biblical message to engage men and meet human needs. Using the Bible as his base and locus, the preacher has been expected to give commentary again and again on its message, with each sermon serving as a document of instruction, inspiration, and witness. Karl Barth highlighted the preacher's role as commentator when he wrote, "It is this man's duty to proclaim to his fellowmen what God himself has to say to them, by explaining, *in his own words,* a passage from Scripture which concerns them personally."[1] That phrase "in his own words" is crucial. It calls attention to the personal context of the sermon as commentary, saying that it is conditioned by the preacher's understanding and use of Scripture, and, as well, by his skills as a communicator.

The sermon is a servant of Biblical meanings applied to human needs. Structured to declare the *kerygma*, restate the *didache,* and promote *leitourgia*, the sermon tradition is a primary means for witness, learning, and worship. The relation of the Bible to all these is indispensable. The relation of the Bible to witness, learning, and worship is indeed so basic that Gerhard Ebeling has commented that "Church history is the history of the exposition of Scripture."[2] The sermon has served a major role in that history.

---

1. Karl Barth, *The Preaching of the Gospel,* ed. and trans. B. E. Hooke (Philadelphia: Westminster Press, 1963), p. 9. Italics mine.
2. A chapter title in Gerhard Ebeling, *The Word of God and Tradition,* ed. and trans. S. H. Hooke (Philadelphia: Fortress Press, 1968), esp. pp. 11-31.

I

As commentary the sermon will reflect the preacher's relationship with the Bible and will present some interpretation of its purposes and claims. Whatever his views may be on some of the leading concepts regarding the Bible—concepts like inspiration, the Word of God, authority, inerrancy—the preacher must have a clear understanding of the function of Scripture in faith and life.[3] His sermons should serve that function. It is this that makes the sermon Biblical.

Some years ago John Knox published a worthy little book on *The Integrity of Preaching* in which he set forth his answer to the question often asked him about what makes preaching Biblical. His book gives a fourfold answer: preaching is Biblical when it remains close to the characteristic and essential Biblical ideas; preaching is Biblical when it is concerned with the central Biblical event, namely the work of Christ; preaching is Biblical when it answers the needs of the Church, nourishing human lives; preaching is Biblical when the central event in a real sense recurs.[4]

The preacher at his best is a transmitter of the Biblical message and meanings, and his sermons are to be preached with an understanding that they are part of a divinely-ordained traditionary process. Albert C. Outler has explained that:

> The Christian Church originated in an act of divine traditioning *(actus tradenti)* at Pentecost—when the apostolic memories were finally transformed into the apostolic kerygma and the loyalties of the disciples of Jesus of Nazareth were transmuted into their faith "that God has made this Jesus . . . both Lord and Messiah." Since that day, the survival of the Church has depended, always at least in part, on the traditionary process by which its time in the world has been prolonged. Tradition, both as act and process, constitutes both the source and the method by which Christians, since Pentecost, have been enabled to know and to respond to the revelation of God in Christ.[5]

---

3. It will be helpful for the reader who has not done so to wrestle with the argument of James Barr, *The Bible in the Modern World* (New York and Evanston: Harper and Row, 1973), esp. pp. 13-34.

4. John Knox, *The Integrity of Preaching* (Nashville: Abingdon Press, 1957), esp. pp. 19-23.

5. Albert C. Outler, "The Sense of Tradition in the Ante-Nicene Church," *The Heritage of Christian Thought: Essays in Honor of Robert Lowry Calhoun* ed. Robert E. Cushman and Egil Grislis (New York and Evanston: Harper and Row, 1965), p. 8.

The preacher who is true to the tradition will reverence the Word he holds and will transmit that Word with honesty, openness, essential fullness, and life-oriented focus.

The New Testament witnesses understood themselves as transmitters, as men entrusted by God to handle and pass on a special deposit of truth. The word they used in referring to that deposit of truth is *paradosis,* a technical term that denotes something of special content that must be handled with concern and obedience.[6] In that word we are reminded of the proper content for our preaching, and we are reminded, as well, of the perspective we need for preparing and assessing our sermons. The merit of our pulpit work rests finally on how we handle the Biblical tradition of truth. Our words have lasting value only as they are based upon God's Word. We preachers are sent by God to say what God wants said, and to say it, as Barth commented, "in our own words." God has placed what He wants said in Scripture, and it is from that source that we must draw our truth, develop our theology, renew our vision, and prepare our message.

II

The Bible is itself a commentary, an extended body of materials treating the theme of God's way with man. Scripture reports the redeeming acts of God in the world of history. That redemptive activity has shaped a special history that is made evident in the Hebrew people, in Jesus of Nazareth, and in the Church. The Bible stands as inscripturated record of the mighty acts of God, and is at the same time a product of those acts. The Bible must be understood in the context of soteric meanings, with both the Old Testament and the New Testament relating to each other in essential correspondence. The New section implies an Old, and both sections demand each other in order to make sense, i.e., hold and bestow meaning. The New Testament provides the history, literature, and theology of the Christian Church, but all of these allude and appeal back to the life and claims presented in the Old Testament materials. Charles H. Dodd has called attention

---

6. See *paradosis,* by F. Buechsel, *Theological Dictionary of the New Testament,* ed. Gerhard Kittel, and trans. Geoffrey W. Bromiley (Grand Rapids: Wm. B. Eerdmans Publishing Co., 1964), vol. II, pp. 172-173.

to how the two testaments relate, showing with scholarly clarity that the Old Testament provides "the sub-structure of Christian theology," because the lines of thought and action in the New Testament are essentially a development of Old Testament promises and themes.[7] The serious preacher will not choose between the testaments for his preaching sources, he will rather keep both testaments related, using some framework by which to honor both in their setting and particularity, whether that framework be the Covenant theme,[8] promise and fulfillment,[9] revelation as history,[10] salvation in history,[11] sacrifice,[12] or some other.[13] Any one of these conceptual frameworks for viewing the testaments together will grant some understanding of the Biblical tradition. There is one problem to be faced, however; none of these conceptual frameworks is adequate in and of itself to explain every feature of life in the testaments. Everything in the Bible cannot be made to fit neatly into one scheme. As we prepare to preach from its vast

---

7. Charles H. Dodd, *According to the Scriptures: The Sub-Structure of Christian Theology* (New York: Charles Scribner's Sons, 1952); see also F. F. Bruce, *The New Testament Development of Old Testament Themes* (Grand Rapids: Wm. B. Eerdmans Publishing Co., 1968), esp. pp. 11-21.
8. See G. Ernest Wright, *The Old Testament and Theology* (New York and Evanston: Harper and Row, 1969).
9. See Bruce, *Development;* A. A. van Ruler, *The Christian Church and the Old Testament,* ed. and trans. Geoffrey W. Bromiley (Grand Rapids: Wm. B. Eerdmans Publishing Co., 1971); Walter C. Kaiser, Jr., *The Old Testament in Contemporary Preaching* (Grand Rapids: Baker Book House, 1973); Elizabeth Achtemeier, *The Old Testament and the Proclamation of the Gospel* (Philadelphia: Westminster Press, 1974), esp. pp. 77-123; Richard N. Longenecker, *Biblical Exegesis in the Apostolic Period* (Grand Rapids: Wm. B. Eerdmans Publishing Co., 1975), esp. pp. 51-103, 205-220; Henry M. Shires, *Finding the Old Testament in the New* (Philadelphia: Westminster Press, 1974), esp. pp. 86-125; Foster R. McCurley, Jr., *Proclaiming the Promise* (Philadelphia: Fortress Press, 1974), esp. pp. 29-65.
10. See *Revelation As History,* ed. Wolfhart Pannenberg, trans. David Granskou (New York: Macmillan Co., 1968).
11. See Oscar Cullmann, *Salvation in History,* trans. Sidney G. Sowers (New York and Evanston: Harper and Row, 1967), esp. pp. 74-78.
12. See Joachim Jeremias, *Der Opfertod Jesu Christi,* Calwer Hefte 62 (Stuttgart: Calwer Verlag, 1963); idem, *The Central Message of the New Testament* (New York: Charles Scribner's Sons, 1965).
13. For volumes reflecting several views, see *The Old Testament and Christian Faith,* ed. Bernard W. Anderson (New York and Evanston: Harper and Row, 1963); *Essays on Old Testament Hermeneutics,* ed. Claus Westermann and James Luther Mays, trans. James Luther Mays (Richmond: John Knox Press, 1963); James Barr, *Old and New in Interpretation* (London: SCM Press, 1966).

commentary on God's way with man, we must wrestle with some evident discontinuities (as well as continuities) that are to be found therein.

The first Christians also wrestled with this problem. Hebrews by background and Jews by faith, they finally parted company with the rest of their Jewish contemporaries when they no longer viewed the Torah as the authority for religious experience and rather saw Jesus of Nazareth, risen from the dead, as the living core around which all religious concerns fall into meaningful place. They increasingly interpreted the major Old Testament themes and meanings by another guiding principle, presumably on the authority of Jesus' own example.[14] In contrast with the rest of the Hebrew nation, explains G. Ernest Wright,

> The early Church obviously did not see Torah in the Old Testament as the most important authoritative element. Instead, the whole literature was read prophetically for the manner in which God had prepared the soil for history's normative event which is the life, death, and resurrection of Christ. Central in the emerging literature to become the New Testament was the passion story of Jesus, together with his words and acts and those of the Apostles, especially Paul, which were commentary on Christ's meaning for church and world.[15]

The culmination of the process of their faith and thought was a theology and literature of which Christ is center. This kerygmatic statement is our theological heritage from the apostolic period and we are under trust to shape our own preaching content and approach by its controlling theme.

Given this heritage of interpretation in the New Testament, we are influenced both by precedent and necessity to view the Bible primarily as a Christological document.[16] By whatever scheme he chooses to follow and unify its multiform materials, the preacher will discover one constant that is central among others: man's need to be related to God in obedient trust. Preaching was ordained to herald both that need and possibility, on such terms of rela-

14. See Bruce, *Development*, pp. 96-99; Longenecker, *Exegesis*, p. 51; R. T. France, *Jesus and the Old Testament* (Downers Grove, Ill.: Inter-Varsity Press, 1971), pp. 223-226.
15. Wright, *The Old Testament and Theology*, p. 180.
16. See Bernard Ramm, *Special Revelation and the Word of God: An Essay on the Contemporary Problem of Revelation* (Grand Rapids: Wm. B. Eerdmans Publishing Co., 1960), esp. pp. 115-118.

tionship as God has willed, and to explain the importance of that relationship for life here-and-now and life hereafter, and the dangers of neglecting it for our lives. Kyle Haselden saw in this theme "The Urgency of Preaching,"[17] because preaching deals with what the Bible deals: "the Peril of God's wrath, the Promise of God's love, and the Option offered to all men in God's Son."[18] The whole Bible offers materials for treating this fundamental theme of salvation. The truth about salvation is thus presented through the use of truths found throughout the Bible. As Bernard Ramm has explained:

> Jesus Christ is the Truth, but we can know him only through the instrumentality of *truths*. Jesus Christ is the living Lord, but we know of this lordship only in the *written* documents of the New Testament. Jesus Christ is Eternal Life, but we know of this eternal life only in the witnessing pages of the New Testament. Only in special revelation do we know that there is a Truth, that there is a Lord, that there is an Eternal Life.[19]

Texts throughout the whole Bible offer truths which point to the finality and importance of Jesus.

The Bible is itself a commentary. It is of a reporting, instrumental character. Correct perspective on Jesus and salvation is presented and determined finally by the whole Bible. If the preacher would see steadily and preach wholly, he must approach the whole book with deep reverence for its literature and teachings, and he must remain increasingly open to serve its purposes and claims. As Paul has written: "All scripture is inspired by God and profitable for teaching, for reproof, for correction, and for training in righteousness, that the man of God may be complete, equipped for every good work (II Tim. 3:16-17). The Church has rightly insisted that its ministers know and preach from Scripture.

III

As commentary, the sermon should reflect a responsible scholarship in the handling of Biblical texts and supportive materials. As for the handling of Biblical texts, the sermon should show

17. Title of his book on the subject (New York and Evanston: Harper and Row, 1963).
18. Ibid., p. 41.
19. Ramm, *Special Revelation,* p. 117.

exegetical soundness. Every text or passage has a central focus as determined by the Biblical writer himself, and although the preacher's final application of the writer's message may occasionally differ from that of the writer, the textual focus must not be violated but valued.

So much has to go into understanding a text. The preacher must come to terms with the writer—his background, milieu, theology, terminology, style. This process is not always easy on him, but the patient exegete-preacher will forever seek to move beyond questions to reasonable answers, beyond general information to specifics, concerned to reach a fruitful understanding and grasp of the materials before him. The careful preacher will do his exegetical work with such interest and integrity that afterward he will readily assume responsibility for linking his sermon with the message intended by the Biblical writer. A sermon is based upon an interpreted text. This means that the sermon can begin to be developed for use only when the content of a text or passage has become clear. In this way the sermon becomes commentary.

The responsible scholarship needed for preaching will often demand additional help beyond the preacher. Although the alert preacher rigorously studies the Biblical materials and grapples with each text and passage in immediate fashion—whether in original languages or translation, there are times when he will need additional tools and helps from Biblical specialists whose skills and competence he does not have. To do Biblical preaching sometimes forces us to deal with Biblical problems,[20] and we need help in seeking to solve those problems and shape a reasonable statement for the pulpit. We cannot always gain fruit by working alone and unaided in the study of the Bible. In wrestling with certain truths, doctrines, themes, texts, characters, commands, promises, etc., we need resources from specialized helper. When this is the case, the preacher can turn unashamedly to those resources for help in his daily study and weekly work.

Standing first and foremost among his preaching resources should be a good translation of the Bible. The choice of a Bible with marginal references and sectional divisions to mark off the change of themes and subject areas is somewhat personal and ar-

---

20. See C. K. Barrett, *Biblical Problems and Biblical Preaching* (Philadelphia: Fortress Press, 1964).

bitrary, but one that recognizes differences of style between prose
and poetry is especially helpful. The specialized aids needed by the
preacher are found in many kinds of literature and many styles
of presentation:[21] journal articles, monographs, various translations
of the Biblical text, grammars, lexicons, dictionaries, concordances,
church histories, biographies and autobiographies, systematic the-
ologies, commentaries on Biblical books, and even sermons from
ancient and modern masters of the pulpit.

It is in his reach for helpful resources that the preacher senses
anew his part in the continuity of preaching and his indebtedness
to those who preceded him in the work. As we open ourselves to
their work, we can expand our range of insights, inform ourselves
about other methods of approach to questions and problems, encourage ourselves to patience in thinking through a matter, and
we can even draw illustrative materials from the past for current
use. There is a vast repository of materials from previous generations of preachers and those materials are readily available to
teach us, refresh our thought, inspire our hearts, guide our thinking, sustain our faith, provide exegetical models, and even correct
our notions. In some instances, we can learn through studying other
preachers and their work how not to do some things, thus avoiding
certain mistakes due to presuppositions and faulty views and emphases.

Every honest preacher will acknowledge his debt to workmen
of the past, to exegetes and spokesmen who by toil and concern
left some record of their thoughtful study and preaching. The commentaries and homilies of the Church Fathers are examples of
such toil and concern; they still hold great teaching appeal in
terms of exegetical methods, theological stress, and applications to
problems and needs then current. A prolonged encounter with
this vast literature can serve to keep us sober, busy, and sane.
Although some aspects of the history reflected in the materials
are now obscure, shining through the stylish mode of such early
works of serious churchmen is an evident studiousness, a love for

---

21. On these aids, see Frederick W. Danker, *Multipurpose Tools for Bible
Study, third edition* (St. Louis: Concordia Publishing House, 1970); David M.
Scholer, *A Basic Bibliographic Guide for New Testament Exegesis,* second edi-
tion (Grand Rapids: Wm. B. Eerdmans Publishing Co., 1973); Otto Kaiser and
Werner G. Kuemmel, *Exegetical Method: A Student's Handbook,* trans. E. V. N.
Goetchius (New York: The Seabury Press, 1967).

the Word and Church, a strong sense of the importance of doctrine to Church life and mission, and an openness to the instruction of Scripture truths. Some of the materials in those commentaries and homilies overlap in emphasis and doctrinal slant, while some other materials differ vastly. In nearly all instances, however, we see basic and profound development of thought, and sometimes the emergence of new elements and fresh doctrinal approaches. With eyes wide open to the history of the preaching task we can see in those volumes the wide variety of gifts among God's chosen spokesmen. Most were men highly talented, thoughtful, enthusiastic about Scripture; the works they have bequeathed reveal them as men of creative drive, compositional skills, expository insights, and meaningful contacts with both the Church and the world of learning. We do learn much from the works of such men.

Consider, for example, the sermons and commentaries of Augustine, where we see some very diverse traditions brought together and used in the interest of Christian truth: one was the intellectual tradition stemming from classical Greek culture, and another had to do with civic interests related to the order of the Roman Empire. Augustine's writings reflect his classical training to be a professional teacher of rhetoric. He knew and utilized the educational values of rhetorical tradition, and he fused that speech culture with Christian doctrine to form a programmatic production in his *On Christian Doctrine*, a book that has had widespread influence across later centuries among men of culture, among them the Venerable Bede and Alcuin. Written during A.D. 397-417, *On Christian Doctrine* deals with the whole matter of preaching, and it is addressed to preachers. Book Four deals with preaching style, while the first three books treat the substance of preaching, which for Augustine had to be Biblical. Although Augustine's study on preaching is not an exact systematic statement, it does reflect his concern for modeling a good Christian homily or sermon. Scholars are still divided in their assessments of how Augustine's theology developed —whether the changes he worked out were major or minor,[22] but there is general agreement that in his preaching the central issue was the proclamation of the Word of God, with the sermon as commentary. Augustine took preaching seriously and prepared for

22. See A. D. R. Polman, *The Word of God According to St. Augustine,* ed. and trans. A. J. Pomerans (Grand Rapids: Wm. B. Eerdmans Publishing Co., 1961), esp. pp. 123ff.

his task with diligence, even equating *Verbum Dei* and *Sermo Dei.*[23]

Augustine's sermons reflect the man's deep thought, his deep feeling, his strict observation, honest reporting about his times, and the pastoral urgency that moved him to prepare and preach. The sermons are generally well-proportioned as to structure, stress, and balance. The sermons reflect that he was aware of the parish needs —and the public and parish sins; that he was sometimes critical, in the prophetic style, sometimes playful, but without joking, sometimes indignant, but without coarseness of manner; that he was always calling attention to the resources of the faith; that he was sometimes elementary in what he said, yet deep in content—meaning that his content was always Biblical in tone and teaching. Over a thousand of his sermons are available for our learning, a remarkable compilation for which we have an exact dating of when they were used (usually in connection with the lectionary).[24] In the sermons and commentaries of Augustine we can see how he kept theology, doctrine, and preaching in basic alliance,[25] an accomplishment to be studied and emulated in our time. Augustine's sermons also show us that he exteriorized his soul in preaching, letting his spiritual experience shine forth freely without any reticence.[26]

The preaching method used by Ulrich Zwingli (1484-1531) is also instructive, especially when viewed in connection with his life. Zwingli was a commentary preacher, which is to say that he devoted his ministry to the work of preparing each sermon as a commentary on some Biblical verse or passage. When Zwingli began his duties as preacher in the Great Minster in Zurich in January, 1519, he boldly announced his plan to preach forthrightly from the text of Scripture, beginning with the Gospel of Matthew. He was resolved to deal with scriptural meanings and thereby bring Zurich under the influence of the Word of God. Although he was perceptive and quick in his thought, Zwingli was not an

23. Ibid., pp. 124, 127. There is an excellent translation of *On Christian Doctrine* by D. W. Robertson (New York: Library of Liberal Arts, 1958).
24. See F. Van Der Merr, *Augustine the Bishop: The Life and World of a Father of the Church,* ed. and trans. Brian Battershaw and G. K. Lamb (London: Sheed and Ward, 1961), esp. pp. 129-198.
25. See *The Preaching of Augustine,* ed. Jaroslav Pelikan, trans. Francine Cardman, The Preacher's Paperback Library (Philadelphia: Fortress Press, 1973), esp. pp. vii-xxi.
26. See Jean Guitton, *The Modernity of Saint Augustine,* trans. A. V. Littledale (Baltimore: Helicon Press, 1959).

outstanding orator. His speech was simple, unadorned, improvisational, and conversational in tone.[27] But that he gave himself to continuous Biblical exposition makes his legacy meaningful for our study. His themes varied, showing concern to relate Biblical insights to contemporary events. A great number of his sermons were addressed vigorously to instill Christian discipline and effect social reform. The study of Zwingli's sermonic legacy will repay the time and effort involved.

There is abundant information and help in the study of the more prominent of Martin Luther's sermons and commentaries,[28] especially that reformer's principles and practices as an exegete.[29] Or, to consider another reformer during the Reformation, there are the resourceful sermons and commentaries of John Calvin.[30] In both instances we are at the fount of a stream that has influenced the continuity of post-Reformation preaching in a major fashion. In both instances we can watch great preachers react to a given preaching tradition and offer contrasting approaches, views, and emphases. The history of preaching has involved varied gifts, different settings, local issues, and universally important concerns.

Ebeling was right: "Church history is the history of the exposition of Scripture." We who preach are particularly influenced by this fact as we study the work of earlier preachers through their published works.

But that history of exposition affects us in still another way: as we study it we discover the sources for much of our present thought and tradition. "The questions and solutions of past generations have seeped into our speech and permeated our thinking in countless ways," as Ebeling has reminded us.[31] We are both

---

27. See Jean Rilliet, *Zwingli: Third Man of the Reformation,* trans. Harold Knight (Philadelphia: Westminster Press, 1964), esp. pp. 57-62.
28. See *Luther's Works,* in the mutlivolumed American Edition, ed. Jaroslav Pelikan (St. Louis: Concordia Publishing House, 1958).
29. See Jaroslav Pelikan, *Luther's Works: Luther the Expositor* (St. Louis: Concordia Publishing House, 1959). See also James Samuel Preus, *From Shadow to Reality: Old Testament Interpretation from Augustine to the Young Luther* (Cambridge, Mass.: Harvard University Press, 1969).
30. See *Calvin's Commentaries,* ed. D. W. and T. F. Torrance (Edinburgh: Oliver and Boyd, 1959). The series is still in process of being translated. See also T. H. L. Parker, *Calvin's New Testament Commentaries* (Grand Rapids: Wm. B. Eerdmans Publishing Co., 1971), an explanatory volume treating the history and features of Calvin's exegetical work. See also Leroy Nixon, *John Calvin, Expository Preacher* (Grand Rapids: Wm. B. Eerdmans Publishing Co., 1930), esp. pp. 47-72, 129-131.

recipients and servants in a fellowship of interpreters, links in a chain of life and work that stretches back from the immediate present into the distant past.

Joseph Parker, famed preacher at City Temple, London, lauded such study of both early and contemporary masters.[32] He admired the strengths of notable Scottish preachers, particularly their solid learning, but he also recognized one of their glaring weaknesses— namely a lack of interest or ability to adapt their style to the mental changes abroad in the land. Those Scottish divines had genius, learning, and experience, but they seemed limited in the ability to reach the popular level of hearers who lacked their learning. Parker regarded America's Henry Ward Beecher, one of his closest friends, as this country's greatest preacher, lauding him as a man "full of soul," a man of careful thought, precise statement, bridled emotion and popular appeal. In a eulogy of the Brooklyn pastor, Parker credited Beecher with having enlarged the whole idea of what constitutes a sermon, and cited his preaching method as "an amazing combination of philosophy, poetry, emotion, and human enthusiasm—all centered in Christ, and all intended to bring men into right relations with the Father."[33] There is much to be learned from one's contemporaries as well as from the Church Fathers and men of the past.

When he was in his middle fifties, Parker announced his in- tention to publish a "preacher's Bible," feeling that his life and thought and opportunities had prepared him well enough for that helpful task. The project was to involve an original treatment of Scripture from Genesis to Revelation, complete with critical notes, sermonic materials, outlines, illustrations, prayers, meditations, and pertinent questions for self-examination by the reader. Parker's extensive project of comment and exposition occupied a major part of his ministry over seven years and in publication filled the compass of twenty-five volumes. Finally titled "The People's Bible," the series of annotations reveals deep insight, careful exegetical and expositional methods, delicacy and tact, as well as a noticeable absence of repetition. His aim was to "leave it to speak to any one in after time who may care to listen to its testimony."[34]

31. Ebeling, *Tradition*, p. 11.
32. See William Adamson, *The Life of Joseph Parker* (New York: Fleming H. Revell Co., 1902), esp. pp. 165-176.
33. Ibid., p. 193.
34. Ibid., p. 168.

Not every preacher is suited to the task of a continuous exposition of the Bible in one pulpit. The Bible was not written in
that fashion and some of its literature does not lend itself to such
strict treatment. Even Augustine, Luther, and Zwingli trembled at
their task—and they went out to their people treating strategic
books and sections of Scripture rather than following a strictly
linear approach. There are strategic books that the preacher should
plan to treat, and given the practical example and help of earlier
exegetes and preachers, he can do a worthy job—with practicality,
variety, centeredness, and timeliness. Even our generation of hearers, conditioned as they are to well-packaged presentations and
never-ending variety available through the multimedia, will respond
in openness to texts and sections of a Biblical book that are treated
with insight and immediacy in well-prepared sermons. When the
preacher does his homework well, considers his audience with
deep concern, and respects the purposes of the Word of God, he
can expect to attract and influence many "who may care to listen
to [his] testimony." Responsible scholarship wedded to spiritual
depth helps to make this so.

Joseph Parker, upon hearing a fellow minister speak disapprov-
ingly of reading the sermons of other men, publicly confessed his
own approval of such reading. Said he:

> There is no kind of literature I enjoy more, and no course
> of reading would do you more good than a course of sermons
> of the fathers of all Churches, who are the sainted dead, or
> the illustrious living.[35]

He added, probably with some stress on the personal pronoun,
"I never cease being refreshed by reading and studying such."[36]

Every preacher owes it to himself to study good sermons; they
help him "turn on." But there are other more demanding reading
materials that stimulate thought, spur creativity, and aid our learning. It is imperative that we read: it helps us to react, to reach
out in thought, and to be renewed.

Reading is not always an easy affair. Some works have achieved
such a vision, such a depth, such a scope, that the reader needs
time, if not assistance, to move about meaningfully in the new
terrain. Such works are a fundamental challenge; the challenge
is to our receptivity, our patience, our perceptivity, our quest to

---

35. Ibid., p. 90.
36. Ibid.

sense truly and understand. Such works disturb our security and test our ability to adapt to new demands. This is especially the case when the author uses concepts and imagery that are barriers until his arbitrary meanings are explained. Those who read theological works reflecting current ferment know this; the same is true of such works as those by Paul Tillich, Rudolf Bultmann, Martin Heidegger, Karl Jaspers, or Alfred North Whitehead, all of whom are monumental thinkers and writers who have framed thought-systems. Some other works, quite apart from any rarefied or obscure concepts or terminology, are not easily understood because they are written in a style that is close and exacting, or expansive and demanding, or actually unfamiliar. At any rate, solid writings fulfill themselves only as they take us under control. We must submit our energies to them before we can receive and react to their ideas. Most solid writings demand and presuppose a wealth of knowledge before the reader can actually see the vision and value embodied in them. The advance occurs only when the reader gives the writer his due, following as the writer guides, meanwhile watching for signposts along the way to identify where he is.

The preacher who reads widely will sometimes acquire a greater sensitivity to Scripture after reading materials that stir him in some way. This is especially the case upon reading those genres of literature which show something more than life as we ourselves experience it. We react by recalling what is fundamental. Our time is rewarded when we read works that lift to our view new dramatic moments, trace out interactions of selves, assess human structures, isolate community concerns, and present forms of challenge that draw us out, prod reflection, sift our intentions, and rebuke our isolation. The preacher must read deeply in his Bible, but he must also read more widely. He must preach the Word, but he is more sensitized to that Word when he has had to react to books and materials that show him life in dramatic focus and raise more questions. One is reminded of Ralph Waldo Emerson's statement that some writings are "vital and spermatic"; that is, they are helpful in getting the mind of the reader into responsible action.[37]

---

37. See *The Complete Works of Ralph Waldo Emerson in Six Volumes,* Current Opinion Edition (New York: Wm. H. Wise and Co., 1926), vol. II, pp. 197, 214; also vol. III, pp. 294-296.

There are times when it is helpful to read writings that show life in scenes to which the preacher must morally and prophetically object. The platform on which the literary fare of the day comes to us is not usually decorated in Christian motifs. Emerson once advised against too quick a dismissal of literature written on what we consider "too low a platform."[38]

> I see not why we should give ourselves such sanctified airs. If the Divine Providence has hid from man neither disease nor deformity nor corrupt society, but has stated itself out in passions, in war, in trade, in the love of power and pleasure, in hunger and need, in tyrannies, literatures and arts—let us not be so nice that we cannot write facts down coarsely as they stand, or doubt but there is a counterstatement as ponderous, which we can arrive at, and which, being put, will make all square.[39]

We should read writings that are psychological instruments, writings that open aspects of experience for vicarious sharing. The minister should know such literature even as it is known by those to whom he ministers, aware that some of them are influenced by the vision of life reflected therein. Knowing the literature (and the vision) he can deal justly with it in the light of Scripture-truth.

Now while all of what has been written above is true and practical for our reading, most of us will readily admit that the greatest reading pleasure lies in religious reading, in writings that deepen our devotion toward God, that lift our minds and hearts to unity with God. When the idea is true, the style apt, the presentation concrete, the vision clear, and the perspective worthy, both devotion and deepening result. One thinks of compilation of prayers, meditational works, poetry, inspirational materials that interest, challenge, interpret, and guide. This kind of writing can carry us beyond formalism and induce spiritual awareness. Wesley confessed that he went beyond formalism only when he found writings that had gone beyond it, particularly William Law's *A Practical Treatise upon Christian Perfection* and *A Serious Call*. Until then Wesley had known only morbid sensitivity, constant introspection, constant search for counsel, and extreme asceticism. But when in 1727 Wesley found those books by William Law, the

---

38. Ibid., vol. VI, p. 201.
39. Ibid., p. 202.

touch upon his soul was direct, then and there, through what he was reading.[40]

E. Stanley Jones has told us that when his book *Mahatma Gandhi: An Interpretation* was first published he thought it was a failure—falling without much obvious impact on the Western world so enamored of armaments. But later, meeting with Martin Luther King, Jr., Jones was commended by King for that book. Said King: "It was your book on Gandhi that gave me my first inkling of nonviolent noncooperation. Here, I said to myself, is the way for the Negro to achieve his freedom."

"Then my book was not a failure," Jones replied.

"No," King answered, "if we can keep the movement non-violent."[41] A new spirit for the struggle had been determined. A new methodology had been decided upon—via solid, perceptive reading.

Most of us will recognize the name and work of Dom Gregory Dix, the great Anglican liturgical scholar. When he was dying he lost all interest in the former things to which he had long given attention, particularly talking to other people and even reading the paperback detective stories that had given him so much delight. Someone brought him a copy of the newly published commentary on St. Mark by Vincent Taylor. Dix examined the new book with interest and was aroused. He was so stimulated by the book that his whole demeanor changed and he resumed conversation with people. Just before he died, Dix conversed about Christ with another patient and was successful in leading him to saving faith. Dix's brother wrote a letter to Vincent Taylor afterward expressing his gratitude for the book, lauding it for what it had done to renew the life and spirit of his dying brother. A book had brought a man out of the doldrums—and had made him an effective agent in the conversion of another man to Christ.[42] Who can predict the final influence of a solid piece of reading?

---

40. See *The Journal of the Rev. John Wesley, A.M.*, ed. Nehemiah Curnock (London: Robert Culley, 1910), vol. I, p. 467.
41. E. Stanley Jones, *A Song of Ascents: A Spiritual Autobiography* (Nashville: Abingdon Press, 1968), see pp. 259-260.
42. A. Raymond George, "Vincent Taylor," a tribute given at the funeral service in November 1968, and published in Taylor's posthumous book *New Testament Essays* (London: Epworth Press, 1970), p. 3.

There are evidences in history that show preaching has improved not only because reading in depth stimulated and sensitized the preacher, but also because the preacher was influenced by the style of what was read. Principal James Denney once confided this about himself to a group of students, quoting it as his wife's recent assessment: "James," she had asserted, "I think your preaching style has greatly improved since you took to reading those French novels."[43] Responsible reading informs, sensitizes, and fulfills us in more ways than one.

There is no mistake about it: our preaching will reflect our understanding and use of Scripture, but that understanding and use are given greater effectiveness when aided and sustained by a solid program of reading. A deep and steady program of reading informs us. It can reinforce our appreciation of those who can stir and guide our thought. It can enrich our store of illustrative materials. It can also show us the power of effective expression.

As for the way reading enriches our store of illustrative materials for preaching, Harry Emerson Fosdick found it necessary once to give an explanatory defense for resorting so often to allusions and quotations in his sermons. "If one thinks of them as intended to be decorative, or even in a popular sense illustrative," Fosdick explained, "my purpose in using them is completely misunderstood." He continued,

> They are intended to be case studies and so a substantial part of the argument. Nowhere are the common frustrating experiences of personal life more vividly described, our familiar mental and emotional maladjustments more convincingly portrayed, than in biographies and autobiographies, poems, novels, and dramas, and this rich storehouse of psychological self-revelation and insight has been too much neglected.[44]

Responsible reading is a must if the preacher is to develop that responsible scholarship needed to sustain a responsible pulpit.[45]

---

43. *Letters of Principal James Denney to W. Robertson Nicoll: 1893-1917,* ed. W. Robertson Nicoll (London: Hodder and Stoughton, Ltd., 1920), p. xxxix. The statement is part of the material in J. A. Robertson's "Memoirs of a Student," which he contributed to that volume.

44. Harry Emerson Fosdick, *On Being A Real Person* (New York: Harper, 1943), p. xi.

45. See James Earl Massey, *The Responsible Pulpit* (Anderson, Ind.: Warner Press, 1974), esp. pp. 68-79.

IV

The crucial questions with which the alert preacher must wrestle every time he has delivered a sermon are: How did I handle the Story? What did I do with the challenge presented in the message of the text? Did I pass on the heritage with fidelity and reverence? Did I show it alive by my work?

Speaking personally, I have found that some of my deepest insights into the handling of Biblical truth came when I, influenced by my previous training to be a concert pianist, began to compare the preaching occasion to aspects of a music concert: "Each concert is an audible answer, sometimes quiet, but sometimes loud, to how we are coping with the 'great heritage,' whether it continues to live"[46]—"great heritage" meaning the classical tradition. How often I have listened to music, my mind alert to both visual and sound memories of the music scores, and tested the artist not so much on precision or finish but on the degree to which his achievement was true to the intentions of the composer. Although there can be a thousand and one differences between pianists—differences in poise, temperament, culture, gestures, guiding conception, forcefulness, projection, art of touch, tonal range, virtuosity, experience, maturity, instinct, and warmth—there is one feature which must be common to all artists in order to serve the purposes of the music, namely fidelity to the composer's intentions. Given that fidelity on the part of the performer, the hearer is helped to catch the message and vision of the music.

It is not hard to transfer this concept to the realm of the preaching task. Preaching succeeds best when true to God's intentions for it, when the preacher stands committed in fact and feeling to the Biblical witness, letting the tradition come through clearly and forcefully and invitingly in his sermon, in "his own words," as Barth put it. The Bible is central for preaching: apart from its message and meanings we fail at the business of criticizing and correcting life, we miss the way of salvation, and remain in the rut of ineptitude.

Continuing with that theme of fidelity, let me draw again on the music world for further insight. During a part of my time of

---

46. Joachim Kaiser, *Great Pianists of Our Time,* trans. David Woodbridge and George Unwin (New York: Herder and Herder, 1971), p. 7.

music study, I was a special student at Salzburg's Mozarteum under Professor Heinz Scholz, a master pianist. Although he was not pedantic, Scholz was a precisionist who watched over my Bach and Beethoven with the meticulous care of the serious pedagogue. Scholz was part of that European tradition in which the music stands first, with the artist subject to its authority and control. Scholz was a stickler for the use of a proper text *(Urtext)* and insisted that his students reflect their knowledge of that text in their playing. There was more at work in his mind than mere academic theory or interest in pianistic purism: he honored the music. Abram Chasins recalls an incident reported to him by his wife, pianist Constance Keene. While on a tour of Germany she heard a Mozart concerto played by a pianist whose performance, in her estimation, was less than adequate for that noble piece. Yet at the close of the concert the audience responded in near wild applause. She was puzzled at this response to what she considered a dreadful performance, especially since the audience was musically educated and experienced. When she asked one of the members of the orchestra about the applause, he, agreeing with her assessment, answered that the audience was applauding Mozart, not the poor soloist![47] Perhaps even churches educated and experienced in Scripture have put up with some poor preaching, yet have reacted warmly to the preacher—because they respect the Word!

Tertullian asserted, referring to the Scriptures, "This property belongs to me." He declared, further, "I am heir to the apostles. As they provided in their will, as they bequeathed it in trust and confirmed it under oath, so, on their terms, I hold it."[48] Martin Luther had to have a sound defense when passing through the storms of criticism. He confessed, "We teach no new thing but we repeat and establish old things, which the apostles and all godly teachers have taught before us."[49] That is the spirit of a preacher true to the Biblical tradition, the preacher who shapes his sermons to give commentary on Biblical meanings in the interest of human needs.

---

47. See Abram Chasins, *Speaking of Pianists,* second edition (New York: Alfred A. Knopf, 1961), pp. 99-100.
48. See his "Prescriptions Against Heretics," par. 37, *Early Latin Theology,* ed. and trans. S. L. Greenslade, The Library of Christian Classics (London: SCM Press, Ltd., 1956), vol. V, p. 58.
49. See Luther's *Commentary on Galatians,* E. T. 20 (1.14).

Bishop Gerald Kennedy reports that when he was a seminary student many years ago he had some worries concerning the ministry, one of which was the fear of running out of fresh and relevant materials to preach week after week. But prolonged exposure to Scripture helped him overcome that problem, so he adds that "time has revealed the miracle of the inexhaustible depths of the Gospel." After preaching for almost fifty years Bishop Kennedy is still excited about preaching, humbly boasting, "If I should live to be a hundred, there will still be a wish for more time to tell more of the old, old Story. There is no other subject in the world a man could discuss several times a week for a lifetime without any sense of repetition or fatigue."[50]

Such is the warm word of a veteran preacher who with many others holds Scripture in reverence, exercises himself in responsible scholarship, and shapes his sermons as commentary on God's way with man.

---

50. Gerald Kennedy, from his foreword to *Best Sermons: 1962,* ed. G. Paul Butler, Protestant edition, vol. VIII (Princeton, N.J.: Van Nostrand Co., Inc., 1962), p. vii. See also Gerald Kennedy, *While I'm On My Feet: An Autobiography* (Nashville: Abingdon Press, 1963), esp. 135-140.

3. *The Sermon As . . .*

COUNSEL

"Wherever a congregation assembles, whatever its size," writes Merrill R. Abbey, "the need for counsel is present." "The sermon is most true to its intended function," Abbey continues, "when it renders real help in meeting specific, identifiable needs."[1] As a functional form of communication the sermon is expected to invite to and grant counsel.

The sermon that counsels is described variously as "life-situation preaching,"[2] "project method preaching,"[3] or "therapeutic preaching,"[4] and sometimes "pastoral preaching," but by whatever description the purpose is the same: to render real and redemptive help to persons with specific and identifiable needs. The needs are as varied as life itself and as deep-seated as its experiences. The sermon that counsels will be spoken to share insights, promote change, provide emotional release, rehearse meanings, answer questions, resolve conflicts, strengthen purpose, appeal to motives, heal inward injuries, stimulate faith and trust, encourage to adventure, and purge the soul, to name only a few identifiable needs among hearers.

---

1. Merrill R. Abbey, *Communication in Pulpit and Parish* (Philadelphia: The Westminster Press, 1973), p. 125.
2. The literature is vast, but see Halford E. Luccock, *In the Minister's Workshop* (Nashville: Abingdon-Cokesbury Press, 1944), esp. pp. 50-92; Charles F. Kemp, *Life-Situation Preaching* (St. Louis: The Bethany Press, 1956), esp. pp. 11-29.
3. See Harry Emerson Fosdick, *The Living of These Days: An Autobiography* (New York: Harper and Brothers, 1956), esp. pp. 92-100.
4. See H. Grady Davis, *Design for Preaching* (Philadelphia: Muhlenburg Press, 1958, esp. pp. 127-138, although the expression is used "with some misgiving."

Sermons that counsel are sometimes called pastoral sermons since they are known to grow out of a pastor's contacts with men in their need and are preached out of pastoral interest for those men. This kind of sermon is marked by earnestness, compassion, a sense of reality, and insight. Henry Sloan Coffin, in reporting by request on his own methods and insights as preacher once confessed, "The most useful sermons come to me as a pastor in visiting the homes of my congregation, or from other contacts with individuals. Their questions or their situations clutched at my heart, and I turned to the Word of God in the Scriptures for an answer. I still find that the most potent stimulus to sermon-writing arises from the experiences through which I see men and women passing."[5] Thus prodded, the preacher's sermonic work is properly termed pastoral in nature and effect.[6]

Harry Emerson Fosdick, who became one of the world's most renowned pulpit spokesmen, acknowledged that he learned how to preach by focusing on the real problems and needs of his parishioners. During the first year or so of his ministry the young pastor floundered while trying to find a preaching method and relevant subject matter. "The seminary's course in homiletics had been of slight use to me," he wrote. "We listened to lectures on preaching, full of good advice, I do not doubt, but lacking relevance to any actual experience of our own, and soon forgotten because not implemented in practice. You cannot teach an art simply by talking about it."[7] Observing the needs of his people, and building upon a speech course he had had as an undergraduate, Fosdick worked out what he termed a "project method" for preaching and steadily gained in preaching ability and effectiveness. Years later Fosdick asked the nation's clergy "What Is the Matter With Preaching?"[8] and outlined his method for correcting the situation. Still later, his project method was widely recognized as a most creative means for dealing in the pulpit with specific and identi-

5. Henry Sloan Coffin, "The Interpreter's Discipline," *Here Is My Method: The Art of Sermon Construction,* ed. Donald Macleod (Westwood, N.J.: Fleming H. Revell Co., 1952), p. 59.
6. For some excellent examples of this pastoral preaching, see Charles F. Kemp, *Pastoral Preaching* (St. Louis: The Bethany Press, 1963), and his *The Preaching Pastor* (St. Louis: The Bethany Press, 1966).
7. Fosdick, *Living,* p. 83.
8. See *Harper's,* July 1928, pp. 133-141.

fiable needs.[9] Nothing can make preaching easy, but the best preaching always offers that which can make the hearer's living easier—and more rewarding.

1. As counsel, *the sermon helps to clarify life.* It can help men handle the confusion that experiences often bring.

The process of clarifying life through preaching calls for dedicated workmanship on the part of the preacher. It calls for a man whose heart is in his work and whose head is in it as well. He must know and understand if he would teach and make clear. He must believe and feel, associate with and relate to men, if he would stir men and lead them to trust. He must grapple with his own "horizons,"[10] dealing with the limits of his own vision, and frankly face his own presuppositions if he would bless his people with vision, extend the horizons of their thought and expectations, and lead them further into truth. The men and women to whom we preach all stand at some point in their experience where we must help them to see, understand, and act with purpose. Counsel by means of the sermon can help them to see clearly, understand clearly, and act boldly with clear purpose.

The clarifying of life will demand the useful exposition of the Word of God. The Psalmist knew this:

> The unfolding of thy words gives light; it imparts
> understanding to the simple. (Ps. 119:130)

Under the influence of the Word of God, a man experiences insight. Given focused explanation and pointed illustration through a sermon based upon God's word to men, a hearer becomes heir to a moment of realized truth.

The real clarifying of life calls for this contact with the Word of God. Release from confusion does not always result from the restatement or rehearsal of the faith of our fathers. The faith of our fathers came from contact with God through His Word and Spirit, and thus it must be experienced to be understood and become effective for us. Harold A. Bosley once commented that "We spend too much time praising the faith of our fathers and

9. See Edmund Holt Linn, *Preaching As Counseling: The Unique Method of Harry Emerson Fosdick* (Valley Forge: The Judson Press, 1966), pp. 11-26.
10. On this concept of "horizons" see Bernard J. F. Lonergan, *Method in Theology* (New York: Herder and Herder, 1972), pp. 235-237.

too little time seeking to understand it."[11] Giving man clarity about
life has to do with granting understanding; it has to do with
the sharing of insight. It means to deal ably with values, alternatives, possibilities, the nature of life, the needs of man, the will
of God. And this understanding grows out of the Word of God.

But the clarity men need has to do also with an obedient
openness to God. Interestingly, Jesus linked knowledge and clarity
about life with commitment to God; he cited obedience and commitment as the way to make sense of life. Every preacher should
read Frederick William Robertson's sermon on John 7:17, the
text in which Jesus said, "If any man's will is to do his [God's]
will, he shall know. . . ." Robertson titled his sermon "Obedience
the Organ of Spiritual Knowledge."[12] Obedience does clarify moral
values and responsibilities. It highlights from within the wisdom
of integrity and safeguards human freedom. D. Elton Trueblood
wrote, "It is not easy to be a human being. Human life carries
with it marvelous possibilities, but there are, at the same time,
untold ways in which it can go wrong."[13] At a time when the
battle of ideas and standards of behavior continues unabated—
and that time is always—our preaching must provide counsel, clarifying life and pointing the way out of confusion.

2. *The sermon that counsels can help the hearer become centered* for a right look at himself and his experiences.

Preaching should help a hearer to see where he is and should
be or what he is and should become. This is why preaching must
state the truth: the truth about life, the truth about human nature,
the truth about the human will, the truth about sin, the truth about
spiritual issues and relationships. The project of centering the hearer depends upon the truth about the hearer as God knows and
gives it through His Word. The process is sometimes painful, for
both preacher and hearer, as when the prophet Nathan confronted
David and with pointed word announced, "You are the man!"
(II Sam. 12:7). Given that convicting word, David shook with
terror, but he finally stepped forward in repentant confession and

---

11. Harold A. Bosley, *Preaching on Controversial Issues* (New York: Harper
and Brothers, 1953), p. 36.
12. Frederick William Robertson, *Sermons Preached at Brighton* (New York:
Harper and Brothers, n.d.), pp. 300-307.
13. D. Elton Trueblood, *The Yoke of Christ and Other Sermons* (New York:
Harper, 1958), p. 11.

acted wisely to let God restore him to favor. This centering is an inward result, and the word of counsel sensitizes the soul to help achieve it.

This is well illustrated in a sermon Paul E. Scherer once preached, "On Facing Yourself."[14] Using a four-point structure, Scherer announced: (1) "The New Testament keeps saying from cover to cover that 'you are your own greatest problem.'" (2) "You've got to see it [self] as it is; and there's only one place for that: in front of Jesus, who is the Presence of God!" (3) "You've got to accept that self of yours, with its blots that the hymn talks about, its conflicts and its fears, its poverty, all the little shams with which it tries to cover up: accept it and surrender it!" (4) "Then you've got to lose it!" With seemly advice born of concern and the beckon of the Gospel, but spoken with pastoral authority, Scherer insisted:

> Forget it somehow! Don't cherish it, and try to live up to it, or down! Don't defend it, and keep patching over the cracks with excuses! Let it go in something that's bigger than you are. . . .[15]

The will of God in Christ, of course! This was sound counsel for persons squirming in self-scrutiny, dissatisfied and disturbed about the self they knew. The Gospel is addressed to such men, and Scherer was using that Gospel to meet that common human need.

Preaching must involve counsel for real needs. Edgar N. Jackson treated this matter quite suggestively about twenty years ago in a book about *How to Preach to People's Needs*.[16] The book was most surely needed and was widely received. Out of his own pastoral experience and clinical expertise Jackson dealt with some areas of human need and offered specific suggestions and sermon models (some from acknowledged pulpit masters) for treating them from the pulpit. Among the many areas of need Jackson discussed were these: how to preach to the guilt-laden, the sorrow-filled, the fearful, the insecure, the lonely, the defeated, the angry, the doubter, the tense, the sick and shut-in, those who feel inferior, those who are gripped by injurious habits, the aged, the immature,

---

14. Paul E. Scherer, *The Place Where Thou Standest* (New York: Harper, 1942), pp. 109-114.
15. Ibid., p. 114.
16. Edgar N. Jackson, *How to Preach to People's Needs* (Nashville: Abingdon Press, 1956).

those having family problems, persons with a drink problem, etc. The list was not exhaustive, nor the book definitive, but the suggestions were apt and timely. Jackson's book provided a good study for preachers eager to learn the "how to" of dealing with human needs through preaching.

3. The counseling sermon does more than clarify life and help the hearer to become centered for committed action; *that sermon also complements life,* providing that powerful plus element associated with the Gospel.

The approach of the preacher must involve something more than the perspective of theory and psychological insights; the resources of the preacher must involve something more than the techniques of speech engagement, identification, and group process. The counsel needed in the sermon stands rooted in the spirit and directives of the Gospel. Only the Gospel has the dynamic which hearers need to become whole, act upon guidance, and fulfill the will of God for their lives. Paul was highlighting this plus element when he told the saints at Rome, "For I am not ashamed of the gospel; it is the power of God for salvation to every one who has faith. . . ." (Rom. 1:16). Our counsel as preachers is more than simple advice. When rooted in the Gospel it is energized by the Spirit as the very counsel of God.[17]

Using as allies the public reading of Scripture, congregational prayer, ancient hymns and spiritual songs, the preacher can help to transform the worship setting into a moment of truth and help his hearers experience a *kairos* before God that is instructive, inspirational, involving, and supportive. "Ideally," writes Harold A. Bosley, "the sermon brings the great affirmations of faith and the great issues of life, like electrodes in an arc light, closely enough together to enable the fire of kindling knowledge, hope, and strength to leap into being. Every preacher strives for this all his life and finds the full reward for living in having had the privilege of attempting it."[18]

4. *The counseling effect of a sermon is assisted most acutely when a sense of community prevails between preacher and people.* Popularly termed "achieving identity" with the hearers, this sense of togetherness is a part of the basic psychology of the preaching

17. See Acts 20:27.
18. Bosley, *Controversial Issues,* p. 9.

task.[19] I have treated this in more extended fashion in an earlier book of mine,[20] but the importance of this element of community needs to be emphasized because a church's concern for the variety value of many voices (several speakers coming and going, from near and far) can sometimes overshadow the counseling value of the pastoral voice.

Something special and deep prevails in the service of worship of a group backed by vital traditions and drawn together by mutual love. There is a unique impact in such sharing. Where there is an interest in each other as sharers, as "members one of another," to use Paul's phrase, and as responsible followers of a common leader, there is the overcoming of isolation and the kindling warmth of community. There is something more at work than social awareness in a group possessed of a common concern and guided by a common leader, especially if it is a religious group and that leader is an acknowledged man of God.

The majority of a church's assemblies are characteristically religious. This is true as to the nature, form, and purpose of the service, whether it be to solemnize a marriage, memorialize a deceased member, dedicate a child, receive communion, or celebrate God in common praise. The integral factor in each instance is religious concern, and it is on that concern that the members are called to concentrate with openness. Given this religious concern, a church group is apparently open to the many revelations expected through the experience of worship. Although the music, the prayers, the praise, and the ritual of public readings all play their strategic part in the service, especially the preaching is expected to be a revealing action. This is not only because the preacher holds a learned relationship with the Bible, the Church's book of revelation, but also because he holds a living relationship with the assembled group. Standing in a formal but loving relationship with his hearers, the pastor's very presence is itself revealing, and on a most intimate level. The preacher-pastor is both representative figure and revelational person. The sight of the pastor is always suggestive of sharing, intimacy, membership, family status, guidance, and personal appeal. No appreciative member will view the

---

19. See Edgar N. Jackson, *A Psychology for Preaching* (Great Neck, N.Y.: Channel Press, Inc., 1961), esp. pp. 63-80.
20. See James Earl Massey *The Responsible Pulpit* (Anderson, Ind.: The Warner Press, 1974), esp. pp. 104-105

pastor merely as a man in general; no, he is always a related person, a man in particular, a parson. Nor are his sermons just sermons in general; they are means of help and healing "for us, and for me." One is reminded of Ernest Fremont Tittle's fame in this regard. During his years at Evanston's First Methodist Church Tittle's preaching audience usually contained a rather large voluntary group of students. The students were not there because he was a college preacher as such. They came because they felt related to Tittle; they believed that he loved them not as students but as human beings. Tittle preached directly to their human needs; he gave them and all others what he called "livable truth."[21] Like other appreciative hearers those students believed that Tittle lived that truth himself, and was sharing it with them as a treasure personally endorsed and bearing their names. Preaching in such a context and by such a pastoral person holds special importance and thrust.

No preaching counsels like that of a pastor, or, to use George A. Buttrick's qualifying phrase, "a man with pastoral imagination."[22] A good pastor is a father to his people, and he serves them in the manner of a parent. There are passages in Paul's writings that both state this relation and grow out of it. Consider I Corinthians 4:14-17. While speaking a word of rebuke, Paul paused to say:

> I do not write this to make you ashamed, but to admonish you as my beloved children. For though you have countless guides in Christ, you do not have many fathers. For I became your father in Christ Jesus through the gospel. I urge you, then, be imitators of me. Therefore I sent to you Timothy, my beloved and faithful child in the Lord, to remind you of my ways in Christ, as I teach them everywhere.

This figure of the leader as a father is used again in Philippians 2:22, part of a statement about Timothy again: "But Timothy's worth you know, how as a son with a father he has served with me in the gospel." In I Thessalonians 2:11-12 Paul speaks about

---

21. See Halford E. Luccock's introduction to Ernest Fremont Tittle, *A World That Cannot Be Shaken* (New York: Harper, 1933), esp. pp. ix-x. See also Robert Moats Miller, *How Shall They Hear Without a Preacher? The Life of Ernest Fremont Tittle* (Chapel Hill: University of North Carolina Press, 1971), esp. pp. 141-161, 243-271.
22. George A. Buttrick, *Sermons Preached in a University Church* (Nashville: Abingdon Press, 1959), p. 7.

his concern for that congregation and its affairs, reminding them, "for you know how, like a father with his children, we exhorted each one of you and encouraged you and charged you to lead a life worthy of God, who calls you into his own kingdom and glory." In each setting we have before us a family style relationship and an expectation of mutuality among the members.

The analogical significance of the image of father for pastoral work and preaching is crucial. As leaders we are expected to exercise the care and concern of a father for the congregational members; like children in a family setting they need attention and help for growth and guidance. Fathering as an agent of the Lord among his people, the pastor must be ready to nurture, protect, encourage, stimulate, give a sense of Christian culture, and guide them in the development of competencies. Our counsel is important to these ends. We must seek to prepare the church environment with which our members have to live. We must ably interpret that environment and its meanings to the members, and we must guide their interaction with that environment. We do all of this in the spirit of caring and wield our influence in fatherlike fashion. The pastor who cultivates the spirit and style of a good father will not lose his reward—nor his church. When his preaching reveals his love and apt counsel, it will be a major reason why he remains loved and valued.

This concept of the pastor as father is still strongly influential in the Black Church tradition which shaped my life. In our tradition the preacher's leadership is spiritually necessary and psychologically strategic. The black congregation stands or falls by the kind of fathering the preacher makes available through his life. It might well be said that in some cases, perhaps the majority, when members leave a black church it is due primarily to disorders or deficiences in relating to the preacher rather than problems with anyone else in the church!

W. E. B. DuBois, in a very perceptive essay "Of the Faith of the Fathers" in his book *The Souls of Black Folk,* eulogized the black preacher and his unique leadership role among his people. "The Preacher is the most unique personality developed by the Negro on American soil. A leader, a politician, an orator, a 'boss,' an intriguer, an idealist,—all these he is, and ever, too, the centre of a group of men, now twenty, now a thousand in number."[23] As preacher to the flock, the black minister is also a father figure, "the centre of a group," nurturing, binding the family through his contacts and commitment, guiding the members in growth, encouraging them in distress, and assisting them in the development of faith and competencies. These are parental functions and they reveal the worth of a father.[24] Our Black Church tradition still honors this image, although we do not see our use of it as an isolated or exclusive pattern. A part of the strong sense of church membership among blacks, however, must be credited to the family concept in our church life.

Our training, time, work, experience, and fathering abilities come through in our preaching. We do not leave these behind as we ascend the pulpit stairs; no, all these feed what we have to say, and they influence the very way we say it. They influence our perceptions, nourish our empathy, and sharpen our discernment. These factors all help to guide us in both the preventive and curative concerns out of which we plan our preaching.

Gaining assurance about the way to counsel through preaching is not an overnight matter. The process is both costly and time-consuming. We develop suitable methods from the lessons of experience, trial and error situations, and a growing knowledge of our people. There are times and subjects when our treatment can be direct, but there are times and problems when an indirect preaching approach is wiser. Despite any experiences we accumulate, however, there are some choices of method that God Himself must dictate to us.

As regards the direct or indirect preaching approach, the differences betwen them can be illustrated by the ways in which books are opened when new. One way, that used by book lovers and librarians, is what I call the "first-things-first method." In this procedure the new book is taken in hand, placed on a table or desk with its spine or binding down. The front cover is then pressed down on the table, then the back cover the same way. The pages of the book are held in one hand while a few are opened and pressed down in the back, then a few in the front are given

23. W. E. B. DuBois, *The Souls of Black Folk: Essays and Sketches* (Greenwich, Conn.: Fawcett Publications, Inc., 1961), p. 141.
24. On this, see especially Erik H. Erikson, *Insight and Responsibility* (New York: W. W. Norton and Co., 1964), p. 129.

the same treatment. The process continues in alternating fashion until the center of the book is reached. When this has been done a few times, the book pages thereafter open freely.

The other method can be called "forcing the issue." This is the quick and sure way, but alas, the more damaging. The book is seized in both hands, pressed firmly against the desk top, with some of the pages held tightly in one hand and the rest of the pages in the other, the two sections being pulled down and outward. The book opens, yes, but the binding is often broken and split because it has been forced.

Preaching to meet certain human needs calls for wisdom in knowing which method to use at any given time. The first-things-first approach is the more logical, usually; it honors the hearer's intelligence and appeals to his judgment. I referred earlier to the word of Nathan the prophet in confronting King David about his adulterous sin against Uriah. Nathan used the first-things-first approach: he began in an appealing manner, with a parable, then worked his way toward the center of David's life. The story readied David for the unsuspected sting through his own interest in the details. Although Nathan's "You are the man!" struck the king at his inward center, the guilty monarch's "binding" was still intact. The counsel smote his conscience but with saving concern. Here was counsel that disturbed a man in order to deliver him.

I recall a certain counseling sermon I preached to deal with religious prejudice among some of my congregation who were rabidly conscious of denomination. These were members whose view of the Church narrowed to involve only those who looked, spoke, and acted like themselves—and bore the same church name! I set myself to correct that stance by duly informing them about God's Church. I knew that my counsel would be a "hard saying," so I softened my critical friends with a bit of humor. I told of being aboard an airplane with my wife. The preparation for take-off was being made in the pilot's cabin, while the stewardess was making her routine announcements about safety precautions to us back in the passenger cabin. "Please extinguish all cigarettes, return your tray tables to their original and upright position, and fasten your seatbelts." One fellow was sitting just ahead of Gwendolyn and me on the other side of the aisle, reading, too preoccupied (or perhaps overly familiar with such instructions) to hear, and his book was propped up on the tray table in front of him.

I said to my wife, "People just don't listen anymore; they're too preoccupied!" The stewardess saw him, noticed that he had not heard her, and repeated herself in a courteous tone—then finally had to move down the aisle, touch the fellow on the shoulder and break his preoccupation. She smiled as she raised his tray table and fastened it to the back of the seat in front of him; then I heard her ask him, quite kindly, to fasten his seatbelt. I watched it all, somewhat amused, but also a bit disgusted. Meanwhile the plane was being backed out from the entrance ramp. I was still watching the other passengers as the stewardess checked on fastened seatbelts. Then as she came down the aisle toward where Gwendolyn and I were sitting, I shuddered! Looking down I suddenly realized that I had not fastened my seatbelt! Just as she was about to say something to me, I grabbed my belt, hooked the ends quickly, then looked up at her with a kind of half-guilty smile! Preoccupied! Judgmental! And also blind to my own fault!

The congregation roared with laughter at my confession. Just as the laughter ebbed away, I said, "This also happens in religious matters." And without lengthy elaboration my point was made. By their own admission, some members have regarded that sermon as their mirror and means for a corrected view. At least many learned that we can also be wrong by default! It was a case where humor helped the counsel.

D. Elton Trueblood's book about *The Humor of Christ* was the outgrowth, he tells us, of an experience in the home when his oldest son, then aged four, started laughing as a certain Scripture passage was being read. After the initial shock, the child's reaction, when understood, became a revelation. Trueblood afterward watched for signs of humor in the sayings of Jesus, and discovered many. He also discovered that some sayings of Jesus seem to make sense most immediately when understood as a joke form, so to speak, while they seem out of place and even damaging unless viewed in this light, that is, as humor designed to convey truth. Writing recently about the reception accorded that book Trueblood reports, "The book has been the occasion for many letters from total strangers, who have reported that they have been helped by seeing Christ in a new light and thereby have been freed from a false stereotype."[25] Occasional humor softens hard counsel. (I

25. D. Elton Trueblood, *While It Is Day: An Autobiography* (New York and Evanston: Harper and Row, 1974), p. 77.

have found that a bit of humor has sometimes served to free me from being the victim of a false stereotype in the eyes of some who hear me preach.)

5. There is yet another observation to be made about the counseling sermon: *it gains in effectiveness when our words and style are in keeping with what we seek to convey and do.*

There are times when the substance men gain from what we say depends in large part upon how we say it. As preachers we make an impact and wield an influence through the contagion of presence, manner, and sound. I have often asked myself, before preaching, How must Jesus have sounded when He taught some of His most crucial doctrines or shared His most sensitive counsel? How must Jesus have advised "Love your enemies and pray for those who persecute you"? (Matt. 5:44b). He doubtless spoke with a positive command, matched by a sufficiently serious facial expression to mark His wisdom. He must have so spoken that no hint of fear was given, nor any suspicion aroused that this was but a coward's strategy to protect Himself. "Love your enemies. . . ." Jesus must have advised this with such gravity as not to appear naive. He must have spoken that line imaginatively, but with a distinctive reserve to show openness on his part to discussion about it afterward. The new program of life Jesus outlined to His hearers had to be attractive to them; He therefore matched the sense of His statements with the spirit of His life and the sound of His voice. "Love your enemies and pray for those who persecute you." He must have uttered that "strange word" and "hard saying" with deliberateness, letting the hearers hang upon each aspect as but an extract from a larger store of instruction. To read the sayings of Jesus is to see a preacher at work whose speech was serious, judicious, inspirational, exacting, but sometimes softened for easier hearing by well-placed humor.[26] Much of the recorded preaching of Jesus is of a pastoral nature, counseling and inviting to counsel. His truth was not always self-evident, but insinuated itself and its meaning into the lives of His hearers. Jesus took care in couching His counsel. He vocalized his vision in attractive, arresting speech patterns: rhythmic lines, alliteration, parables, aphorisms

---

26. On this, see D. Elton Trueblood, *The Humor of Christ* (New York: Harper and Row, 1964).

and proverbs, metaphors and similes. Every form was to serve a function—the cure of souls; and without those carefully constructed forms that function would have been poorer in its immediacy and impact.

Let us make no mistake about it: the way we couch our counsel and voice our vision will greatly influence how we are heard. All sermons, all speech, really, will forever involve two levels, essential meaning and emotional impact. Both levels of hearing are fundamental because the express requirements of using words must involve both at one and the same time. Preaching at its best will always hold these levels in relation, well aware that sense, style, and sound must "work together for the good" of reaching people from the pulpit.[27]

It is now time to summarize and conclude this theme. As a means of public counsel, the sermon is expected to help clarify life for the hearer. As a useful exposition of the Word of God it grants understanding and insight. By means of its counsel a sermon helps to center a hearer, allowing a right judgment about himself and his life in the light of God. The sermon that counsels also complements life, making available to the hearer the power for life inherent in the Gospel. The counseling effects of the sermon deepen when preacher and congregation are in close relation under God. And to see himself as fathering among them helps the preacher in his actions among and acceptance by his church family. The counseling sermon also gains in effectiveness when our words and style say emotionally what our content says essentially.

"No one can exaggerate the opportunity given to a preacher," said John Watson, "when, on the morning of the first day of the week ... each man carries his own burden of unbelief, sorrow, temptation, care, into the House of God, and the preacher has to hearten all. ..."[28] The concerned preacher pays "his bitter premiums to experience"[29] in learning how best to do this, but when he does his work with interest—

27. On this, see Dwight E. Stevenson and Charles F. Diehl, *Reaching People from the Pulpit* (New York: Harper, 1958), esp. pp. 73-82.
28. John Watson, *The Cure of Souls: Lyman Beecher Lectures on Preaching at Yale University 1896* (New York: Dodd, Mead and Co., 1896), p. 5.
29. Ibid., pp. vii-viii.

> Both heart and head—both
> active, both complete,
> And both in earnest—[30]

he will generate the affection and sense of alliance that are basic for helping persons. Most surely should our sermons assist this ministry.

---

30. Elizabeth Barrett Browning, from *Aurora Leigh*.

4. *The Sermon As . . .*

CREATION

Sermons are created things. They grow by process and plan. A sermon is the product of a homiletical mind and a pastoral heart working together to shape an idea of truth for public hearing. The appeal of a sermon rests largely on its substance (or content), its shape (or logical structure), and its spirit (or presentation). Since these factors have been treated in earlier chapters,[1] it is now time to discuss that all-important creativity by which the sermon process begins, continues, and fulfills itself.

I

The creation of a sermon begins with an idea. The idea can result from observation, congregational life, personal experience, or reading. Every preacher will recall sermons prodded by all these but might also find that one area of stimulation is far more appealing and fruitful than the others. Dr. W. Dale Oldham confesses that he has found the best stimulation for his sermonizing in good books. "All a preacher actually needs for a sermon is a good idea. Reading the right books provides those ideas."[2] Every preacher knows just what it usually takes to "prime his pump" and get him going, what stirs him to react and act with the pulpit and his people in mind.

---

1. Although chapter I includes some treatment of sermon presentation, there will be more on that topic in chapter V.
2. W. Dale Oldham, *Giants Along My Path: My Fifty Years in the Ministry* (Anderson, Ind.: Warner Press, 1973), p. 215.

Beginning with an idea, the sermon process can be traced in three main stages. First there is the level of impact—the idea registers itself and stirs us to thought. Second, there is the level of an activated imagination. Finally there is the level of intention as to the use of the idea.

When we ask the question about how a sermon is made, we are really asking about the nature of any creative act, because "creative activities, irrespective of medium, exemplify a common pattern," as Harold Rugg has explained.[3] The logic of any creative act always involves impact from some idea or experience; and with an activated imagination that works freely to deal with what has been discovered or discerned, something new emerges. Creation begins when one's exposure to life leads to an engagement between mind and possibility, and a will to express ourselves about that engagement. The sermon is the preacher's main organized way of expressing insights and impacts which he has from life and God.

The second level—that of activated imagination—is especially crucial for sermon development. Unless the preacher's imagination becomes fully engaged, nothing meaningful happens; but once the imagination has been stirred, then everything becomes possible. There is a very perceptive word on this matter of aroused imagination in one of the chapters of the late Jesse Jai McNeil's book on *The Preacher-Prophet in Mass Society*. In giving that word McNeil sought to distinguish between the elements of sightseeing and mind-seeing.

> To look long, steadily, and precisely at an external fact is to experience the gradual formation of perceptions which lie behind the thing itself—perceptions which are the result of the mind seeing deeper meanings than the objectivity of the external fact.[4]

Both seeing and feeling are basic ingredients for the fruitful work of the imagination, but hard work is demanded to train ourselves to see with discernment and chart the internal results once we have been stirred by what the external order has presented to our seeing. The best sermons begin when eye and mind relate in a

---

3. Harold Rugg, *Imagination* (New York and Evanston: Harper and Row, 1963), p. xiv.
4. Jesse Jai McNeil, *The Preacher-Prophet in Mass Society* (Grand Rapids: Wm. B. Eerdmans Publishing Co., 1961), p. 86.

seeing that becomes an experience of impact stirring the imagination to its fruitful business.

Beginning as the product of an impact, the sermon is itself in turn shaped to produce an impact. It begins as a product of experience and it fulfills its purpose by producing an experience. The sermon begins in a context of felt "undergoing," which is one of the conditions under which imagination is engaged. As John Dewey has explained, "There are conditions to be met without which an experience cannot come to be. The outline of the common pattern is set by the fact that every experience is the result of interaction between a live creature and some aspect of the world in which he lives."[5] As for the preacher, he lives his life within two impact-producing worlds of experience—the Bible and life. and from both his sermons can take their rise and undergo development.

What is being said here, then, is that the sermon is an influenced product; it does not just happen without antecedents. The impact of an idea or insight into a text, a phrase, a clause, a word, or an experience, can begin a whole program of thought. A sermon develops in substance from the germ of the motivating idea we caught. The idea attracts, engages, and influences us. If the idea is intense in its impact and suggestive in its applicability, its character bids us to lay hold upon it for use.

II

Granting the commentary character of the sermon, and affirming the Bible as the source of our preaching themes, the creative work of sermon building is helped immediately through choosing a text or passage. Life has a way of opening us to certain texts, just as certain texts have a way of opening us to life. George A. Buttrick once explained that it makes little difference whether the preacher chooses his text or a text chooses him[6]—so long as the sermon is Biblical in the end. Or to cite Buttrick's wise words again,

"[Texts and subjects] are not found: they come of themselves.

5. John Dewey, *Art as Experience* (New York: Capricorn Books, 1958), pp. 43-44.
6. George A. Buttrick, *Jesus Came Preaching: Christian Preaching in the New Age* (New York: Charles Scribner's Sons, 1931), p. 152.

They jump from between the lines of the book you are reading, though it may be a very secular book. They look out at
you through the mirror while you are shaving. They write themselves on the wall of the house across the street. They tremble
in the glow of evening prayer."[7]

James T. Cleland also agrees that it makes no difference whether
the preacher begins his work with Scripture or with a human situation, explaining, "It makes no difference, so far as content is concerned, provided he remembers that he must deal with the other
also before he words his sermon."[8]

In beginning with a text the wording of the sermon is greatly
aided by the wording and mood of the text itself. If the preacher
has discerned the Biblical writer's pattern and understood his style—
applying the requisite criticisms (textual, linguistic, literary, historical, etc.),[9] he should feel the movement of the writer's thought
and catch the impact of the writer's message and insight. That
message and insight then provide the central matter with which
the preacher is to work. A sermon is the logical, sequential, and
unified handling of textual meaning, and to this end all sermon
sections and sentences are to be prepared. If the preacher has
discerned the Word of God in its dignity in the text, he will also
experience a sense of drama from the impact of its truth. It is
not hard to create when there is discernment and drama.

I have been speaking about the Word of God and the writer's
message, thought, and style. Interestingly, every text with which
we deal in confronting Scripture has this "double identity," as
George Eldon Ladd terms it. "The double identity of the Bible
as both the Word of God and the words of man is an amazing
phenomenon; and it is easy to forget or to overlook one aspect
or the other."[10] The word God sent was brought by men; the word
God sends in preaching is shaped by men. The sermon is that
shape and form. It has an instrumental character that is "an amazing phenomenon" of creation, a creation in which both God and

---

7. Ibid., p. 149.
8. James T. Cleland, *The True and Lively Word* (New York: Charles Scribner's Sons, 1954), p. 71.
9. On these, see George Eldon Ladd, *The New Testament and Criticism*
(Grand Rapids: Wm. B. Eerdmans Publishing Co., 1967); Norman E. Perrin,
What Is Redaction Criticism? (Philadelphia: Fortress Press, 1969).
10. Ladd, *Criticism*, p. 83.

man work. God suggests and prods; the preacher receives, reacts, shapes what is heard, and preaches it.

So much depends on the preacher's ability to shape what he sees and hears in the Word. Quite often the Biblical writer's form of presenting his message both opens our eyes to what he is saying and gives a clue as to how to shape it for restatement in sermon form.

1. As regards writing forms, consider *narration*. Among the many styles for presenting the Biblical message, narration occupies the chief position. The reasons are not hard to find, and they are readily understood. Narration (and the need for it) arises out of our basic humanity within the historical process.[11] It is a way of organizing and presenting life; it is a way of re-presenting events, situations, happenings, and tracing cause-effect realities. Narration grows out of the innate desire we all feel to trace experience in some sequence—since life itself is lived in that way. Narratives help us to see the substance of experience, focusing more centrally on life than any other forms of presentation allow. Narratives help us to discern the logic of life, drawing meaning out of movement. Narratives are both framework and focus, device and teaching. They give us a pattern for perspective. The sequences in narration tend to telescope time, granting us the leisure to rethink and relive and review—and be renewed through re-presentation of meanings. In this way, narratives help us to discover and affirm identity, exciting interest in a possible experience through appeal to our concern for process and control. Narratives and stories excite hope. They show us ways of relating. Narratives and stories interrogate us and put a case before our attention. Narratives and stories can warn, encourage, and motivate. It is not by accident that so much of our Bible is in narrative form.

There is more in the Biblical narratives and stories than the expression of culture, although culture is certainly involved there.

11. On this, see Stephen Crites, "The Narrative Quality of Experience," *Journal of the American Academy of Religion,* vol. 39, no. 3 (September 1971), pp. 291-311; Harald Weinrich, "Narrative Theology," *The Crisis of Religious Language,* ed. Johann B. Metz and Jean-Pierre Jossua, trans. Francis McDonagh, Concilium Series (New York: Herder and Herder, 1973), pp. 46-56; Ted I. Estess, "The Inennrrable Contraption, Reflections on the Metaphor of Story," *Journal of the American Academy of Religion,* vol. 42, no. 3 (September 1974), pp. 415-434.

There is more in that form than the authority of the past. There are insights in the narratives, messages in the action, truths opened in the portrayals, wisdom in the climaxes. There is feeling and appeal in the form. Because form and feeling are so inseparably conjoined in them, narratives and stories can become signals of the sacred—as when Jesus used them. The Gospels cite this as His characteristic preaching method (Matt. 13:34b; Mark 4:34a).

No preaching succeeds so well as an alert, informed, inspired commentary on some Biblical narrative. It is a thing of inspiration to watch an informed speaker working away happily on a story, "telling the Story"—as we say in the Black Church tradition, affecting the hearers by ancient art and for cause. When the preacher has a talent for handling detail; when he has worked his way through complex portrayal of an event to seize centralities in the happening; when he has imagined his way into the minds and motivations of the characters, studied the links between actions, and observed well the writer's transitional items; when the time, place, happening, and effect have produced a dominant impression on the preacher's mind and spirit—so that he can enlarge and focus our understanding in a climax of that impression, then our listening has not been in vain. Narrative preaching can give lift and life, and break through barriers—as did the parables of Jesus.

Narration calls for a talent in the handling of facts, sequence, and timing. Given the conclusion in the narrative passage, the preacher has just what he needs to grant him focus and the singling out of his aim and theme. In working out the plan of presentation the preacher must keep the style of treatment subordinate to the spirit and scope of the passage. He must let what is central in the narrative remain central in his sermonic restatement. He must have an active imagination in working over the reported happening, but must at the same time saddle that imagination with the fixed safeguards of honest reporting, plausible conjecture, and decent embellishment. This makes the sermon truthful while dramatic, thoughtful but down-to-earth.

The late Peter Marshall had a talent for the use of narratives in the pulpit. He saw himself doing his best when he was engaged in pictorial preaching, helping his people to see. Said he, "What we have to do is to take a passage of Scripture and so carefully and accurately reconstruct the context of it that the scene comes to life. We see it first ourselves. Then we take our listeners to the spot in imagination. We make them see and hear what happened so vividly that the passage will live forever in their minds and hearts." Marshall added, "It's like a newsreel from the Scriptures ... a film from the world's big drama."[12] Instances of his work to this end are his books of sermons, *Mr. Jones, Meet the Master*,[13] and *John Doe, Disciple*.[14]

2. There are considerable riches for preaching to be found in the Biblical *dialogues*. The Bible is filled with dialogues that yield great insight for sermonic use and many thoughtful, hard-working preachers have discovered and used them well. How those dialogues are put to use reflects both the preacher's insight and "outsight," as it might be called, his perception of Scripture meanings and his purpose as he faces and addresses his hearers.

George Arthur Buttrick preached a very perceptive sermon based on the dialogue between Jesus and the father who wanted his epileptic son healed (Mark 9:14-29). Rightly viewing verse 24 as the pivotal line of the dialogue, Buttrick used it as his basis for preaching about "Faith and Doubt."[15] His grasp of the basic thrust of the dialogue stands revealed in the total sermon, but the summary of the case and the way he gathered up the contemporary concerns of his hearers stand out clearly in Buttrick's statement: "The man confessed his doubts and faced them ... cleaving, nevertheless, to his faith."[16] That able university preacher was encouraging Harvard students to give their doubts to God. Knowing by pastoral closeness and professional care just where those students were at a particular crux in history, Buttrick gave them a word from Scripture appropriate to their situation and need. That text served him well—and through his penetrating concern to gain and shape its insight Buttrick served the interests of that textual passage quite well also.

12. Peter Marshall, *John Doe, Disciple,* ed. Catherine Marshall (New York: McGraw-Hill Book Co., Inc., 1965), pp. 124-125. The statement is part of a conversation between the Rev. David Simpson and Peter Marshall during their seminary days; Simpson shared the reminiscence in a letter to Catherine Marshall after the death of her husband.
13. Peter Marshall, *Mr. Jones, Meet the Master* (New York: Fleming H. Revell Company, 1949).
14. See footnote 12.
15. George A. Buttrick, *Sermons Preached in a University Church* (Nashville: Abingdon Press, 1959), pp. 23-29.
16. Ibid., p. 28.

There is an interesting pericope in Mark 7:24-30 that contains a dialogue between Jesus and the Syrophoenician woman pleading for him to heal her afflicted daughter. It is more than the story of that woman's faith; it is also a story about caring across boundaries. It is a lesson on human relations. Quite similar in spirit to the story of His conversation with the woman of Samaria (John 4:5-30), this story reflects the way Jesus dealt with outsiders, so-called. The preacher must live with this story until its real treasure is seen, and must go beneath the surface of the words of the story if he is to discern the true attitude of Jesus toward non-Jews. A surface reading of the passage might give the impression that Jesus spoke to the woman with a prejudicial attitude, defending the limitations He had set for His ministry, but that dialogue does not teach this at all.[17] As I have stated in dealing elsewhere with this story (but from the Matthaean parallel: 15:21-28):

> Did he not insult her by calling her a "dog"? Did Jesus only intend to test her? If so, was this not an insulting way to test her? Did he not delay when she first spoke to him, as if he was not interested in her case? The statement of the evangelist is quite plain: "But he did not answer her a word" (v. 23*a*). Why was he so hesitant? Because she was a Canaanite and [he] held himself back in reserve as a Jew sent on mission to Jews? The woman doubtless thought this when Jesus finally spoke to her as he did, "It is not fair to take the children's bread and throw it to the dogs?" (v. 26). Did she really have to *win* his sympathy? Was he reluctant to help her? There is so much that the account does not tell us, but it is of interest that Jesus' words to the woman—while admitting the limited ministry to which he had been committed—were not actually insulting in tone or meaning: he did not speak to her using the word for dogs that roam the streets, annoying, obstinate, and unclean; he rather referred to non-Jews as little puppies who were house pets. It was a tender touch about an evident distinction with which the woman was certainly familiar; her reply to his statement makes it clear that she was familiar with the distinction.[18]

17. See Vincent Taylor, *The Gospel According to St. Mark: The Greek Text with Introduction, Notes and Indexes* (London: Macmillan and Co., Ltd., 1952), pp. 347-351.
18. See my *The Hidden Disciplines* (Anderson, Ind.: Warner Press, 1972), p. 77. On the distinction between the Greek terms for dogs, see *kuon* and *kunarion*, by Otto Michel, *Theological Dictionary of the New Testament*, ed. Gerhard Kittel, trans. Geoffrey W. Bromiley (Grand Rapids: Wm. B. Eerdmans Publishing Co., 1965), vol. III, pp. 1101-1104.

Jesus risked the usage, trusting that she would sense the tenderness He felt through the softer word He offered—a warm word that showed His difference from other Jews, a kind spirit of evident openness to non-Jews. There is plenty here to give insight for preaching about problematic race attitudes and stereotypes.[19]

The subtlety in that story is not immediately apparent because the dialogue is generally used to illustrate the importance of persistent faith. The subtlety in the dialogue between Jesus and Nicodemus (John 3:1ff.) is also often missed because the story is usually separated from John 2:23-25, to which it rightly belongs as an explanatory illustration of the fact that Jesus "did not trust himself to them, because he knew all men ... [and] what was in man." That dialogue with Nicodemus does teach about the new birth, to be sure, but it is basically an example, vivid and concrete, that Jesus was not fooled nor misled by calculated appearances and sly approaches.

The dialogues of Scripture are highly suggestive and useful. They hold great insight, and that insight must be tapped. In sifting any dialogue one must watch the details of the scene and setting, the persons actively engaged in the action, and the subject or topic under discussion. The stance of each speaker must be understood, and much of that stance is revealed—sometimes subtly— through the techniques employed by each speaker. The outcome of the dialogue always holds a lesson; and so do the intentions of the evangelist or writer who thus used and preserved the accounts.[20] In sifting any dialogue for its teaching and thrust for preaching, it is wise to ponder what application can be made of it beyond that of the Biblical reporter.

3. The material in the New Testament *letters* is not always as easily handled as the narrative accounts; nor is it always as immediately interesting, although it is basic for teaching. It must be remembered that the letters were sent as substitutes for the personal presence of the writers. Given this background fact, the

---

19. For a helpful volume of sermons addressed to this problem, see *The Pulpit Speaks on Race*, ed. Alfred T. Davies (Nashville: Abingdon Press, 1965). See also *Sermons in American History: Selected Issues in the American Pulpit, 1630-1967*, ed. Dewitt Holland with H. V. Taylor and Jess Yoder (Nashville: Abingdon Press, 1971), esp. pp. 502-522.
20. See Joachim Rohde, *Rediscovering the Teaching of the Evangelists*, trans. Dorothea M. Barton (Philadelphia: Westminster Press, 1968).

studious preacher will read beyond the conventional form to discover the personal levels within the letters.[21] He will search out
implied dialogue, shared tradition, common interests, and the immediate concern. He will weigh the writer's stresses, rehearsals of
event and meaning, and watch the way in which the writer appeals
to the church members to heed his message and unite together
spiritually. First person references will not be overlooked. Ethical
teaching will be charted and compared with materials found elsewhere among the writings. The letters are imperative as preaching
resource, filled as they are with instruction, ethical focus, con-
fessional materials, and the basic Christian world-view. All of these
elements combine to reflect what Robert W. Funk has termed the
basic "intentionality"[22] behind and within the letters.

The sermon is an influenced product; it does not just happen
without antecedents. Faithful study of the Biblical materials keeps
the preacher alert to essential accents, and to a wide arena from
which to develop sermons. As Buttrick has well put it, "Many have
never found the Bible too narrow a pasture."[23]

A recent study of the late Albert Schweitzer's sermons called
attention to his homiletic prowess, particularly to his ability to
explore and expose a text with clarity and centeredness. "In particular he allowed himself to be led by the picture suggested by
a word."[24] The sermons in his posthumous collection titled *Reverence for Life* reveal quite clearly that that many-sided giant of
the mind and spirit was "a man of concrete imagination and perception rather than of abstract thought."[25] Schweitzer was a close
observer of Scripture and preached from great texts. An excellent
example of his ability to grasp basic insights and expose them in
his own words is his sermon "Reverence for Life," from which the
book of sermons was titled. Based on Mark 12:28-34, that sermon

21. See William G. Doty, *Letters in Primitive Christianity* (Philadelphia:
Fortress Press, 1973); and still earlier, Amos N. Wilder, *The Language of the
Gospel: Early Christian Rhetoric* (New York and Evanston: Harper and Row,
1964), esp. pp. 39-43.
22. Robert W. Funk, *Language, Hermeneutic, and Word of God: The Problem
of Language in the New Testament and Contemporary Theology* (New York
and Evanston: Harper and Row, 1966), esp. pp. 237 (note 53), 248, 296ff.
23. Buttrick, *Jesus Came Preaching*, p. 146.
24. Ulrich Neuenschwander, "Albert Schweitzer as Preacher," editorial post-
script in Albert Schweitzer's *Reverence for Life*, ed. and trans. Reginald H.
Fuller (New York and Evanston: Harper and Row, 1969), p. 150.
25. Ibid., p. 152.

is a perceptive condensation of the meaning of the love command. It is also an illuminating exposition of that meaning as an ethic for life.[26] Biblical insights influenced Schweitzer's thought about life, and his questing mind explored the wide ranges within those insights as he sought and found parallel openings to vision in his experience. The deeper he lived, the deeper he looked, particularly into Scripture, and the more powerful and penetrating his preaching became.

Recalling his time as preacher at St. Nicholas Church, Strassburg, Schweitzer wrote, "But to me preaching was a necessity of my being. I felt it as something wonderful that I was allowed to address a congregation every Sunday about the deepest questions of life."[27] His preaching still lives because he drew answers to those questions from the insights of Scripture. Sermons structured upon Biblical insights are of lasting interest because they deal with the elemental and essential. Sermons created by identification with declared truth can be trusted to retain timeliness and bear an eternally contemporary character.

Some preachers have demonstrated a rare ability to deal aptly with all the forms mentioned above—narratives, dialogues, letters, and some forms not dealt with here (parables, proverbs, poetry, and symbols), relating Biblical insights to contemporary needs in good preaching style. Charles Spurgeon was one such preacher. So was Joseph Parker. G. Campbell Morgan belongs to that noble company, and George Arthur Buttrick as well. These men were not only masters of pulpit discourse, they were masters of Biblical thought. Theirs was a preparation broadly based, and an openness to Scripture that was immense. Although a sermon might be found here or there among each man's treasury of preaching that could raise from someone a question or two, the usual handling of their textual material stands as something exemplary from which we can and should learn. As for the men cited, in the majority of instances one can readily see that the themes, structure, and substance of their sermons reveal their essential openness to and dependence upon Scripture for their creative work. Each man let the meaning and mood of the text guide his thought and planning. And each man became known as a Biblical preacher.

---

26. Ibid., pp. 108-117.
27. Albert Schweitzer, *Out of My Life and Thought: An Autobiography*, trans. C. T. Campion (New York: Henry Holt Company, 1933), p. 36.

The truly Biblical sermon is one in which the text and its meaning influence the entire creation, even to the points of topic, structure, and stress, and not just as a "first paragraph" item, as Ernest Fremont Tittle described it. Tittle once observed that he had noticed "that some preachers who always take a text do not always allow the text to take them beyond the first paragraph."[28] Tittle said he believed that the use of a text can save a situation even if the sermon itself is poor. As he said in an address to some seminarians:

> It is not easy to take a great text, or a poor text, and build an entire sermon on it. But it pays off in the end. The sermon is far less likely to be superficial and thin. And after its delivery the people though they may forget—they usually do—what you have said, may remember the text all the rest of their life and derive much benefit from it.[29]

III

The creation of a sermon begins with an idea but stands completed as an improvisation on the insight that the idea has bequeathed. A sermon grows in connection with the preacher's ability to improvise on the theme, topic, or text he has chosen.

As for improvisation, as I like to term it, the process has to do with the way the preacher organizes the idea for presentation. The whole result is a fresh treatment of the text, a new creation that is rich in meaning but is blessed as well with personal overtones. It is a process by which the soul of the preacher mates with the substance of his text. It is this that constitutes the individuality of preaching. It is this that explains why one man can produce a sermon that develops a text with comparative simplicity, while another man, though using the same text, can create a sermon that is of considerable sophistication. The differences are due mainly to personality factors. Intellect, temperament, gifts, and training predispose us all toward singularity, difference, and uniqueness.

A good illustration of this is found in the differences between

28. See Robert Moats Miller, *How Shall They Hear Without a Preacher? The Life of Ernest Fremont Tittle* (Chapel Hill: The University of North Carolina Press, 1971), p. 178.
29. Ibid.

the way Phillips Brooks (1835-1893) treated Exodus 14:30 and
the way Martin Luther King, Jr. (1929-1968), handled that text.
Brooks titled his sermon "The Egyptians Dead upon the Seashore."[30]
He treated that theme in somewhat simple fashion, using short,
crisp, straightforward sentences; there was a bare minimum of
embellishment. King's approach and treatment was philosophical.
He used as his title "The Death of Evil upon the Seashore,"[31] and
his sentences were filled with rhetorical flourishes through adjec-
tives, figures, and dramatic techniques characteristic of "black
preaching."[32] Both men began with a short statement about the
picture presented in the text. Brooks exclaimed:

It was the end of a struggle which had seemed interminable.[33]

King announced:

It was the end of a frightful period in their history.[34]

But in moving on to treat the fact that conditions which seem
permanent have a way of being changed when God so determines,
each man's sermon reveals his own spirit and style.

These two sermons, both based on the same text, show us at
once the nature of improvisation in the creation of a sermon. Both
Brooks and King were seminary-trained and possessed the requisite tools for exegeting the textual passage; but as each man did
his work under the impact of the meaning, he found that something personal happened to transform the text into a new structure
for pulpit use. That personal factor is seen in the differences between Brooks and King at the level of words, sentence style, paragraph thrust, and total structure. The audience and time difference
between the two men must be considered also, but the basic point
here has been made. Improvisation is the key to fresh treatment
of texts, and it is the necessary element for sermon structuring.

Improvisation, as used here, is an art. It is a way of elaborating
on the textual idea and insight. The word is used more familiarly
in the world of music but is surely applicable to the craft of
sermonizing. In both music and preaching, improvisation takes place

---

30. Phillips Brooks, *Selected Sermons*, ed. William Scarlet (New York: E. P.
Dutton, 1950), pp. 105-115.
31. Martin Luther King, Jr., *Strength to Love* (New York and Evanston:
Harper and Row, 1963), pp. 58-66.
32. See Hortense J. Spillers, "Martin Luther King and the Style of the Black
Sermon," *The Black Scholar* (September 1971), pp. 14-27.
33. Brooks, *Selected Sermons*, p. 107.
34. King, *Strength to Love*, p. 60.

from a given point of origin and given text.[35] Something of fixed
form and meaning is redeveloped, expanded, opened to view, while
the basic insight maintains control over the creative agent.

There was a time in the history of music performances when
the virtuoso violinists and pianists had to prove their musical prowess through feats of improvising on certain standard repertoire.
Franz Liszt was an acknowledged master at this. Although he
was a showman, catering to theatrics more often than not, his
playing was generally contagious and compelling because he in-
vested it with "soul." His published transcriptions of Bach, Paga-
nini, and Verdi, among others, reveal his gifts in this area. In that
day, improvising was a matter of public demand, and therefore a
matter of course. Improvising was a way of finding and showing
freedom within a set form, adding flourishes to expose the depth
of a given piece. The end result in the hearing was a sense of
immediate realization, felt urgency, and the impact of newness.
All of this deepened the respect of the audience for the musical
tradition.

Jorge Bolet, a master pianist of our time, has commented about
some of the great pianists he has heard through the years. He remarked about the rich pianism of Josef Hofmann, saying "Hofmann
always gave the impression that he was improvising whatever piece
he was playing."[36] Bolet was really saying that Hofmann's playing
exuded freshness, charm, color, that it was characterized by lyric
flow, high suggestibility, and rhythmic infection—all within the
framework of the given text. Hofmann helped Bolet to feel the
life of the text because it was alive to him.

Personal handling of Biblical insights can effect the same results in sermons. Fixed meanings need not lack freshness for those
who know them. Old texts, often heard, are hardly ever exhausted,
however familiar they have become through use. Classic passages
can be reexplored under thoughtful guides and found to yield increased appeal and power. The preacher is the mediator, and much
of what is possible for the hearer rests within his hands as the
interpreter.

35. In music, improvisation can be understood in two ways: (1) creating in
the absence of notation (non-Western view) and (2) working creatively with
a given notation (Western view). See Bruno Nettl, "Thoughts on Improvisation: A Comparative Approach," *The Musical Quarterly,* vol. LX, no. 1
(January 1974), pp. 1-19.
36. Gregor Benko, "Jorge Bolet," *Stereo Review* (July 1972), p. 57.

But the preacher must see newness before he can shape his sermon to show newness. He must feel the flow of life in a textual passage before he can react with wonder and an active imagination. The line between text and truth must fade or recede, letting him move from sight to insight. There is a level of scriptural meaning that can be discovered by reason; there is a still deeper level that can be known only through a full inner response of soul. Clumsy outlining is sometimes an error of faulty logic, but lack of insight or clarity of idea is usually due to hurriedness—failure to linger with holy things. Sermons that would have an express connection with the texts they seek to treat must be shaped through intimacy with those texts. The sermons must grow from the seeds of truth planted in the preacher's heart through reading in depth. Creativity works best when it deals interrogatively with what is given. We see only when we take time to look at what is there. And, as always, that seeing opens new elements of meaning to view.

The text is given. We who preach, and would do it well, must work within the Biblical materials—exegeting. We must work from the materials—exposing. We must work beyond the materials— applying the insights. Sermon creativity is sparked by exposure of ourselves to what can activate us inwardly. It is fulfilled when a topic and treatment have been produced which can attract and activate those who hear us preach.

IV

Learning to see meaning, and how to shape it logically for presentation is helped quite often by a study of pulpit masters and their methods. John Henry Jowett (1864-1923) confessed to some younger preachers-in-training that he kept himself toned for exacting study of a text by looking at it from the viewpoint of other preaching notables. While in the study, he said, "I ask,—how would Newman regard this subject? How would Spurgeon approach it? How would Dale deal with it? By what road would Bushnell come up to it? Where would Maclaren take his stand to look at it? Where would Alexander Whyte lay hold on it?"[37] Such a practice, Jowett said, always broadened and enriched his own

---

37. John Henry Jowett, *The Preacher: His Life and Work* (New York: Harper and Brothers, Publishers, 1912), p. 127.

conception as he viewed a text, because by looking at it from so many angles "some things appear which I should never have seen had I confined myself to the windows of my own mind and heart."[38]

Jowett went on to warn those seminarians to maintain their own sense of individuality, whatever their limitations, and not be overwhelmed after consulting other minds, however great and renowned.[39] The warning was apt and necessary. It was apt because the very nature of preaching demands a high sense of individuality since the preacher must dispense what is his own, and he must dispense it in his own way. The warning was necessary because every preacher must learn to stand on sleepless sentry duty on guard against the perennial temptation to borrow, plagiarize, imitate, or slough off by repeating others. Learning from others is a law of life. Observing the ways of others, especially pulpit masters, does broaden our own views and feed our needs. But we must not observe others to our own disparagement and cowardly negate our own worth. It is one thing to learn from another, and quite another thing to be locked up in another man's greatness. A sense of limitation should prod us to learn; it should not rot our will to use what we learn. "God knows what is in men," wrote John Lowe, "and uses them as they are, but also overrules them and makes them different."[40] That difference should not lead to timidity nor pride, but to thankfulness and performance.

The influence of preachers upon each other is proverbial. Any honest and appreciative man will thank God for those by whose fire he gained warmth and light, and he will admit the fact—as Jowett did. It is quite possible that Martin Luther King, Jr., gained his inspiration to deal with Exodus 14:30 after reading Phillips Brooks's sermon on that text. I cannot be sure of this, however, and I never got to ask King about the genesis of his own sermon "The Death of Evil upon the Seashore." Not very much has been left for us in print about King's sermonic processes, nor did he make any extensive statement about the sources of his sermon ideas. It is possible that King's sermon was influenced by that of Brooks without his even remembering where he was first stirred by that powerful insight.

This happens again and again in the lives of preachers. Some-

38. Ibid., p. 128.
39. Ibid.
40. John Lowe, *Saint Peter* (New York: Oxford University Press, 1956), p. 9.

thing strikes us and sets us to thinking with full consciousness about how it all began. Or something stealthily insinuates itself into our thinking, without apparent connection with any conscious observation, and hardly betrays its influence until a new creation is upon the heart and mind. This happens to writers. It happens to artists. It happens to sculptors, musicians, poets. It happens to all who create. The mystery of creation is not merely in its multiphased processes, but also in its genesis. No creative person has escaped unconscious influences upon his work.

Joseph Yasser, writing about musicians, commented, "One might assert that not a single composer, even the greatest, has completely escaped the influence of his predecessors and often his contemporaries."[41] Yasser has discussed this assertion using the theme of Rachmaninoff's Third Piano Concerto as his primary illustration.[42] If Yasser's research is accurate, it appears that the mature composer was influenced in the creation of that theme by an old Russian Orthodox chant used in the vesper vigil liturgy which he had known as a child. Although differences can be discerned between that chant and the new form in Rachmaninoff's concerto, there are significant similarities between them, and a common germinal cell. We have here a permutation of melody. Rachmaninoff was once asked about the possibility of such a relationship between that chant and his creation, but he remembered no such influence. He discounted any conscious association, asserting, "It simply 'wrote itself.'" A man of prodigious memory might be expected to remember such influences upon what he consciously shaped, but —if Yasser's claim is correct—this is another instance of unconscious influence upon the creative process, a factor conditioned by humanity with its limitations. This is a problem that can be understood and readily excused.

Every man who preaches should seek to be just as sure as Rachmaninoff that what he has shaped is honestly his own—even if he is unmindful of hidden levels in his work. Any man who honors his own calling and individuality wants to shape and deliver a living thing; he wants his own study, understanding, insight, personality, and flavor to be projected in his pulpit work. Just as

41. Joseph Yasser, "The Opening Theme of Rachmaninoff's Third Piano Concerto and Its Liturgical Proto-type," *The Musical Quarterly,* vol. LV, no. 3 (July 1969), p. 313.
42. Ibid., pp. 313-328.

he would feel dishonored by living in another man's shadow, he would feel dishonest in offering a sermon to God that is not his own creation. As part of his action in worship, the sermon must be the preacher's own if it is to be accepted as a worthy gift. Industrious preachers know this, and they give themselves to their task with concern to be honest, creative, ready, and individual. Such industrious workmen will eagerly light their sermonic fire wherever they can, but they will burn only their own fuel.

There are those in our time who are arguing, however, against such a strict discipline as unrealistic and unnecessary because of the pressures of church and social demands upon our time and skills. This fragmentation of the ministry has been ably treated in many studies,[43] and every minister's struggle to gain or maintain wholeness and depth is an open secret about which very little more needs to be said. Among the many prescriptions offered to deal with the problem of macerated time, particularly as it affects our preaching task, is the open use of borrowed sermons. There is nothing new about this notion, however. It is a well-known fact of history that Samuel Johnson was a recognized homilist—as well as lexicographer—who also wrote sermons for other ministers (John Taylor, Hervey Aston, and William Dodd among them).[44] Johnson wrote sermons well, wrote them quickly, usually for profit and on request: ministers who bought the sermons from Johnson thought that they needed his cast of mind and breadth of pedagogy! After paying one or two guineas for a sermon, the purchasing minister would take it to the desk, copy the sermon in his own hand, after which Johnson would destroy the original as they both watched. Augustine commented earlier in his *On Christian Doctrine* about this kind of practice. He approved of it in some cases because it was by consent, and because he believed that some preachers would

43. See H. Richard Niebuhr, with D. D. Williams and J. M. Gustafson, *The Purpose of the Church and Its Ministry* (New York: Harper, 1956), esp. pp. 48-94; Robert S. Paul, *Ministry* (Grand Rapids: Wm. B. Eerdmans Publishing Co., 1965), esp. pp. 13-68; Seward Hiltner, *Ferment in the Ministry* (Nashville: Abingdon Press, 1969), esp. pp. 15-48.
44. See James Gray, *Johnson's Sermons: A Study* (Oxford: At the Clarendon Press, 1972), pp. 7-9; John Hawkins, *The Life of Samuel Johnson* (London: Printed for J. Buckland, J. Rivington, 1787), pp. 391-392; James Boswell, *Life of Samuel Johnson,* ed. George Birkbeck Hill (New York: Bigelow, Brown and Co., Inc.), vol. III, p. 206.

have a better sermon to present to their hearers than if they tried to prepare one purely on their own.[45]

James Boswell cited some advice Samuel Johnson gave in a letter to a young clergyman who presumably lamented his own poverty of ideas or abilities to make and deliver sermons frequently. After advising carefulness in determining the sources from which he might borrow in his attempt to create, the letter continued:

> My advice, however, is that you attempt, from time to time, an original sermon; and in the labour of composition, do not burthen your mind with too much at once; do not exact from yourself at one effort of excogitation, propriety of thought and elegance of expression. Invent first, and then embellish. The production of something, where nothing was before, is an act of greater energy than the expansion or decoration of the thing produced. Set down diligently your thoughts as they are, in the first words that occur; and, when you have matter, you will easily give it form: nor, perhaps, will this method be always necessary; for by habit, your thoughts and diction will flow together. . . . The composition of sermons is not very difficult: the divisions not only help the memory of the hearer, but direct the judgment of the writer; they supply sources of invention, and keep every part in its proper place.[46]

The advice was apt. It needed only to be matched by the young preacher's alertness and industry.

Joseph E. McCabe wrote recently to commend the prescription of using borrowed sermons.[47] After explaining the values of exchanging sermons with those who purposively agree to shape and share them, the need to repeat sermons occasionally, and the wisdom of borrowing sermons—with acknowledgment to the listening congregation, McCabe cites what he calls "The golden rule: Do it sparingly, and be sure your people know it."[48] Says McCabe, "The myth in the pew is that preachers already borrow freely, which they do not. The myth in the study is that preachers should not borrow at all, which they should."[49] In this way, McCabe asserts, the preacher can avoid repetitions, one-sidedness, and gain help in his writing and speaking style.

---

45. Augustine, *On Christian Doctrine* IV. 29.63.
46. Boswell, *Johnson*, pp. 495-496.
47. Joseph E. McCabe, *How To Find Time for Better Preaching and Better Pastoring* (Philadelphia: Westminster Press, 1973), pp. 59-96.
48. Ibid., p. 96.
49. Ibid.

It is not necessary to defend again the merits of creativity through personal application and disciplined response to the Word of God. Every man yearns for creative freedom. Individuality prods us to attempt it. A divine call to preach encourages it. Intelligence is a gift in that direction. Every congregation expects it, and God rewards it.

V

Every preacher will work somewhat differently in shaping the sermon for delivery. Some will work out the entire sermon in the mind first, then make written notes of a limited kind which they may or may not carry with them to the pulpit. Some others will make an outline of lead sentences and write out the supporting illustrations and quotations in full. Still others feel that they must refine the sermon by writing out all of its parts in full. So much depends upon the preacher's desire, discipline, or bent of mind, and what it takes to have a sense of readiness for delivery.

A sermon is a product of intense thought, a creation whose meanings involve more than what can be left to chance. It should be based on an insight from Scripture and possess a structure adequate to convey that insight with impact and clarity; yet it must also hold a certain tension of thought that allows psychological and "soul" rhythms between the preacher and his hearers. Because of all this the preacher must take care to study well, think clearly, feel deeply, and speak for interest, readiness, and full assurance. Whether with or without a manuscript or notes, the preacher must approach the pulpit with a full mind and heart having predetermined what is to be said, why it should be said, and how.

The proper shaping of a sermon takes its toll upon every preacher's time. Try as we may, it is difficult to side-step the thrust of this weekly demand. Some wisely reserve a strict portion of each day for sermon work. This regular privacy allows the preacher to store away what he will need later and to stir up what was stored away earlier. This storing and stirring is a basic rhythm for pulpit readiness. The storing feeds that silent, unseen process for which the subconscious is responsible; the stirring is to examine the stages of sermon growth in that process. Sermons grow from seeds planted in the soil of the mind and heart. Acted upon by the preacher's inwardness those seeds mature in accord with a timetable peculiar to circumstances and individual creativity. If he has had rich and intense experiences, if he has remained both prayerful and thoughtful, if he has remained open to God and in touch with his people and their needs, the preacher can trust the laws of creative development to work together to his timing and God's glory.

Sermon development is conditioned by our individual inwardness as blessed by our exposure to God and life. So much depends upon what might be called here the "feltness" of experience. As Reginald C. Butler has explained in commenting about creativity in another connection: "For the creation of a vital work of art involves a release of emotional tension, and where no such tensions exist the roots of art do not exist either."[50] Creativity demands far more than planned isolation, however regular or guarded. So much depends upon what happens within the preacher during the withdrawal time. Imagination, emotion, drive, and a sense of purpose must be at work within the preacher's daily life if his sermon planning is to be apt and timely.

Speaking of timely, there is an anecdote, supposedly authentic, about a certain preacher who had unique gifts for having his sermons ready. While on the way to the church where he was to preach one evening he had the company of a young member of the home at which he had been entertained. The walking companion used the time to ask the preacher about some of the reports that circulated about him. One had to do with the preacher's way of selecting a text and determining a subject at almost the zero hour, sometimes while in the pulpit during the first part of a service. When asked about this the preacher admitted that this was sometimes his way, and soon shocked his questioner by asking him to suggest a text to be used that night. There was an understandable pause: the request had fallen upon startled ears. But at last something came to mind. It was a fragment of a Scripture verse, probably recalling a devotional reading that day: "The Lord spake unto Moses and unto Aaron, saying. . . ." That was all. But, true to report, that preacher saw depth in that fragment and commended his young walking companion for the suggestion. According to

50. Reginald C. Butler, *Creative Development* (New York: Horizon Press, 1962), p. 11.

the story the preacher preached that same night on how God reveals his will to listening men. According to Richard S. Storrs, who cited the story, that sermon was in "every way timely and effective."[51]

Most preachers will confess that they do not possess this spontaneity but need to have much more time for shaping a sermon. They will also confess their need for periodic solitude for close study and uninterrupted, sustained thought.

Edgar DeWitt Jones (1876-1956), long-time pastor and noted preacher, wrote about his methods as a sermon craftsman. He was responding to inquiries from other preachers about his methods. Jones told of how he "brooded over texts, Scriptural passages, and subjects upon which [he] planned to preach."[52] He placed great stress upon the importance of "the brooding process," as he called it.

> I have long cherished quiet, uninterrupted hours for this brooding process, and somehow have managed to keep my preparation periods inviolate, even during the ministry of large city churches.[53]

The proper shaping of a sermon takes its toll upon the preacher's time, but the time needed must be allotted if the preacher is going to be adequate.

The time of sermon preparation is more immediately fruitful if one has captured something during other periods of the day, with notations to preserve the yield and stir the mind again. Jonathan Edwards in his younger years worked out a good way to occupy his time profitably while journeying. Interestingly, "he worked out a plan for pinning a small piece of paper to a given spot on his coat, assigning the paper a number and charging his mind to associate a subject with that piece of paper." Then upon reaching his study Edwards would transfer the thought represented by each slip of paper to a larger framework.[54] Edwards sometimes studied and sermonized thirteen hours a day, writing as

---

51. Richard S. Storrs, *Preaching Without Notes* (New York: Dodd and Mead, 1875), pp. 96-99.
52. Edgar DeWitt Jones, *Sermons I Love To Preach* (New York: Harper, 1953), p. 11.
53. Ibid.
54. Elizabeth D. Dobbs, *Marriage to a Difficult Man: The "Uncommon Union" of Jonathan and Sarah Edwards* (Philadelphia: Westminster Press, 1971), pp. 67-68.

he thought and planned for his pulpit. For most of his ministry Edwards used a manuscript in the pulpit; he wanted to say precisely what he meant rather than lose time in rambling.[55] He therefore left us many sermons and serious studies. "He wrote to be clear in preaching," says Ralph G. Turnbull.[56] Thus Edwards's symmetry, orderliness, design, and clarity.

VI

The creation of the sermon does demand ideas and insights, but the growth of those ideas and insights is blessed and made easier when the preacher has a sense of identification with those who are to hear it. Facts must be handled in relation to faces, and lines of truth must be matched with the lives of men. All of this keeps the sermon on center.

There is a climate for creativity when the preacher thinks feelingly about appreciative hearers, when he can recall how what he has said helped to bring clarity, change, and betterment to some needy person. There is profound encouragement to preach when we can see and know fruit from our labor. There is also the rich incentive to preach when we remember those whose words helped us to believe in our abilities, including the ability to guide others. Our powers do not tend to flag so easily or become inert when creative relationships exist between preacher and congregation, providing a climate of acceptance and incentive to live and work with freedom.

Peter Ainslee once confessed that "if in the preparation of a sermon or an article my mind did not work with ease, I would put on my hat and make a round of calls to come back with messages seething through my brain."[57] There are ways for preacher and congregation to be partners in preaching other than stated times for dialogue about preaching.[58]

---

55. See Ola E. Winslow, *Jonathan Edwards: 1703-1758* (New York: Macmillan Co., 1940), pp. 135-137; Ralph G. Turnbull, *Jonathan Edwards: The Preacher* (Grand Rapids: Baker Book House, 1958), esp. pp. 18-20, 42-51.
56. Turnbull, *Edwards*, p. 44.
57. Finis S. Idleman, *Peter Ainslee, Ambassador of Good Will* (Chicago: Willett, Clark and Co., 1941), pp. 46-47.
58. See Reuel L. Howe, *Partners in Preaching: Clergy and Laity in Dialogue* (New York: The Seabury Press, 1967), esp. pp. 76-99.

John Henry Jowett always kept identification with the hearers in his planning:

> When I have got my theme clearly defined, and I begin to prepare its exposition, I keep in the circle of my mind at least a dozen men and women, very varied in their natural temperaments, and very dissimilar in their daily circumstances . . . real men and women whom I know: professional people, trading people, learned and ignorant, rich and poor. When I am preparing my work, my mind is constantly glancing round this invisible circle, and I consider how I can so serve the bread of this particular truth as to provide welcome nutriment for all.[59]

No sermon succeeds like that preached for those with whom the preacher feels himself in vital relation. The church that provides a climate of respect, acceptance, and love, which frees the preacher for work on the highest level, is usually rewarded with work done at that level. Preaching thus becomes an act of love for the people as well as an act of worship to God. It stands to reason, then, that dissatisfaction between preacher and people can dull or deaden creativity; and when there is no positive agreement, the preparation of sermons can hardly be a happy task. William Wordsworth once explained about poetry that "all good poetry is the spontaneous overflow of powerful feelings"—allied with a modifying and directing thought.[60] All good preaching is essentially the same. All good preaching is done by one possessed, as it were, possessed by feeling and fervor allied to serve the interests of Biblical truth and human need. Central to this whole context is a sense of identification with those to whom the message must be given and shared.

Reuel Howe tells about a certain church in Philadelphia which at one time had a succession of great preachers whose work quite overshadowed a later pulpit incumbent. After only one year he was assessed by the pulpit committee as woefully beneath the expected standard of preaching. Upon learning this that preacher offered to resign. But the committee was a wise one: instead of accepting the man's resignation the committee members set themselves to help him become the preacher they believed he could be. Comments Howe, "It is tragic that more ministers do not

---

59. John Henry Jowett, *The Preacher: His Life and Work* (New York: Harper, 1912), p. 136.
60. See the appendix, "Wordsworth's Preface of 1800, with a Collation of the Enlarged Preface of 1802," in *Wordsworth and Coleridge, Lyrical Ballads: 1798*, ed. Harold Littledale (London: Oxford University Press, 1911), p. 228.

recognize their creative dependence upon their congregations and find ways to evoke that assistance."[61] Dialogue sessions with selected members of trusted judgment is one such way to gain that help. Other forms of feedback from the church are also constructive and helpful.

We who preach must keep in mind the people for whom our sermons are prepared as well as the purpose behind our calling. This accounts in part for the joy of study and the delight of preaching. When there is a clear grasp of the Word of God and a passionate concern for the people, then the creation of a sermon is never too hard.

Shaping a sermon with people in mind helps to guarantee so many aspects of preaching. For one thing, the sermons remain immediate: they are delivered from the heart and thereby retain an emotional quality along with Biblical integrity. For another thing, keeping the hearers in mind will help the preacher in his choice of words: he will honor the speech level of the hearers and thereby minimize any distance that unfamiliar vocabulary or stilted style would place between them. The listening atmosphere is thus relaxed—even if the preacher might occasionally interject a new word to foster learning, contribute some element of newness to the occasion, or provide a model for his younger listeners.

This way of planning to preach helps further in that the preacher must in the process keep his ear tuned to what he says.

The sermons of Paul E. Scherer had that ear-directed quality.[62] So do those of George Arthur Buttrick, who, for that very reason, was reluctant to print for a reading audience the sermons he had preached to his Memorial Church audience at Harvard University. Buttrick commented, "Sermons in book form run a hundred hazards. The preacher writes for the ear and must now rewrite for the eye," adding that for him "writing for the ear has almost become second nature."[63] Martin Luther King, Jr., echoed the same misgivings when he published his book of sermons *Strength to Love*. King feared that those sermons, prepared initially for

61. Howe, *Partners*, p. 87.
62. See especially Paul E. Scherer, *The Place Where Thou Standest* (New York: Harper, 1942) and *The Word God Sent* (New York: Harper and Row, 1965).
63. Buttrick, *Sermons Preached in a University Church*, p. 9.

96 The Sermon in Perspective

Montgomery's Dexter Avenue Baptist Church and Atlanta's Ebenezer Baptist Church, would hardly hold their own in a larger reading sphere, saying, "A sermon is not an essay to be read but a discourse to be heard. It should be a convincing appeal to a listening congregation. Therefore, a sermon is directed toward the listening ear rather than the reading eye."[64]

James S. Stewart has added a word from his experience, saying that a vision of the people helps to keep the sermon focused.

> This will give your work those qualities of directness, liveliness, verve and immediacy which are so essential. It will prune drastically your involved, elaborate periods, and sternly repress any addiction to purple passages. It will eliminate irrelevancies. It will constrain you to clarify your own ideas. It will urge you to translate abstractions into concrete terms. It will embolden you to use personal forms of address. It will banish the dull and stilted tediousness of the sermon-essay. It will keep the dominant notes of urgency and reality, of appeal for a verdict, sounding unmistakably.[65]

There is something of discipline as well as creativity in the act of keeping in mental touch with those to whom we are to preach.

A well-planned sermon calls for a sense of timing and therefore an economically proportioned flow of words. The sermon is not delivered in a vacuum but in a certain setting. More often than not, it will be accompanied by music and form part of a worship service dedicated to a specifically religious end. All of this demands a sense of timing in the light of place, purpose, and people.

The preacher's flow of words can be economically ordered when there is but one idea and one central concern in the sermon. We are never wise to try to tell it all at one time; we can't even do it, and even if we could the people might not stay to listen. Once the text has been exegeted in the study and the sermon idea has been structured logically for the pulpit, the next great demand is to proportion the flow of words in an economic manner. The idea can have its due impact only if it has been digested, condensed and brought to focus. The point can be put most clearly when the thesis statement is a condensed and economic introduction to the message. Fashioning that sentence is not always easy;

---

64. King, *Strength to Love*, p. x.
65. James S. Stewart, *Heralds of God: The Warrack Lectures* (London: Hodder and Stoughton, 1946), p. 119.

but if we do it, then the hearer has very little, if any, difficulty understanding what he is about to hear treated and applied to his life.

John Newton, one-time slave trader who was converted and became a forceful preacher, once ventured the opinion that "a whole sermon seldom gets through to people anyway; a detached sentence usually does the business."[66] A thesis sentence both outlines that business and keeps the preacher and hearer focused upon it. Through such a sentence the preacher determines his approach, begins his analysis, and proclaims his aim. John H. Jowett prepared for his pulpit work in this manner. He confessed to his listeners at Yale Divinity School that he did not consider his sermon ready for preaching until he could express its theme in a short sentence that was crystal clear.

> I find the getting of that sentence the hardest, the most exacting, and most fruitful labour in my study. To compel oneself to fashion that sentence, to dismiss every word that is vague, ragged, ambiguous, to think oneself through to a form of words which defines the theme with scrupulous exactness,— this is surely one of the most vital and essential factors in the making of a sermon; and I do not think that any sermon ought to be preached or even written, until that sentence has emerged, clear and lucid as a cloudless moon.[67]

As for the importance of having an economy of words, James Moffatt told of being late once for an appointment with Principal James Denney. Having arrived, Moffatt explained to his senior that he had been held up along the way by a local bore who wanted to talk. Denney, recognizing the name of the fellow, replied, "Yes, that man has more words than thoughts."[68] How tragic if the people can say this about our sermons!

James R. Day admired preacher Charles Henry Parkhurst as one "well timed. He comprehends his subject and has no trouble in making you comprehend it, but he does not exhaust it nor himself nor you. You always wish there were more of the same sort. It is a pity that so many preachers spoil their sermons by

66. Cited by Donald E. Demaray, *Pulpit Giants: What Made Them Great* (Chicago: Moody Press, 1973), p. 119.
67. Jowett, *Preacher*, p. 133.
68. *The Letters of Principal James Denney to His Family and Friends*, ed. James Moffatt (London: Hodder and Stoughton, Ltd., 1922), p. xiv.

overpreaching them."[69] He meant using more words than were necessary. Parkhurst knew how to condense and be concise in preaching. Perhaps his work as a daily columnist for Hearst newspapers helped in this regard.[70] At any rate, his style was terse, crisp, fundamental, and non-verbose.

The importance of an economic handling of words which is full of impact and immediate was urged upon me in a quite particular way some years ago. My wife and I were vacationing in Canada and spent a part of our time attending the Shakespearean Festival in Stratford, Ontario. As I studied the musical portion of the festival offerings I took special note of pianist Glenn Gould's program notes. It was hard reading all along, but when I finally reached the last paragraph I was doubly convinced that something was missing—either in my thinking or in his ability to communicate plainly. Here is the last sentence of that final paragraph:

> But if the craving for contrapuntal intrigue, and those principles of motivic elaboration which were discussed in the work of Berg, Krenek, and Schoenberg is not completely sated, I might perhaps mention that all melodic figurations throughout the entire work are derived from one four-note figure which is very prominently displayed at the outset and which, lest I tactlessly slight the reader's perspicacity, I shall leave (in the best Elgarian tradition), enigmatic.

A newspaper columnist must have also had his difficulties in trying to follow that sentence, for in a review released after the concert he referred to Gould's program notes with a bit of disdain. He quoted the very sentence which I have given above, and he added, at the end of his quote, "It is not only enigmatic, it's impossible to figure out."[71] The wording of our sermons must never be so.

An alert, intent preacher will be careful and concerned about word choice and delivery, adapting both in keeping with his style and his hearers. Speaking is a creative action that demands a kind of oscillation in the preacher's mind as he plans the sermon, going back and forth between the store of ideas and the store of words by which it is to be expressed. He is intent on illuminating the

69. James R. Day, foreword to C. H. Parkhurst's *My Forty Years in New York* (New York: Macmillan Co., 1923), p. xiii.
70. See Edgar DeWitt Jones, *The Royalty of the Pulpit* (New York: Harper, 1951), p. 86.
71. Stan Helleur, "You Can Quote Me," *The Telegram* (Stratford, Ontario), Thursday, July 12, 1956, p. 38.

Word, cultivating interest, declaring his message with insight, and thus stirring his hearers to a suggested action. The primary tool for which he is responsible is the sermon—an elaborated, clear, and central statement framed in the preacher's own words. Those words must be ready at hand available, well-chosen, apt, obedient to his call. Words are to the alert preacher like hairs of a fine brush to an artist, all the hairs mingling to the skillful production of the desired picture. Words are like a hand, by which a door is opened to the House of Meaning, bidding the hearer to enter. Word are also like a hammer to a builder, a driving instrument to fix a thought and fasten it securely to the hearer's mind. Conscious planning, then, must stand behind the words, together with a principle of advisability in their use. The making of the sermon with this in mind is the preacher's worship deed and bounden duty.

5. The Sermon As . . .

CHARISMA

The way of a preacher with a sermon is marked out for him by two basic influences: nature and grace. The influence of nature is seen in the preacher's intelect, temperament, gifts, and training. The influence of grace is seen in how these natural factors are enlisted and enhanced by the touch of God. Sermons become charismatic when natural factors and spiritual conditioning together determine them, when they issue from one upon whom mercy and grace have been bestowed granting humanity a set of special benefits through "the participant presence of God."[1] It was to this that Dietrich Bonhoeffer was pointing when he told his seminary students at Finkenwalde that "a sermon is only relevant when God is there. He is the One who makes its message concrete."[2]

The charismatic nature of the preaching task is seen again and again in Scripture. The New Testament explains the power and dignity of preaching under that apt phrase "anointed to preach" (Luke 4:18; Acts 10:38), linking together in vital fashion the service of preaching with the fact of prior selection by God to do so. Luke's interest in this theme is well-known,[3] and it is he who

1. See Wayne E. Oates, *Christ and Selfhood* (New York: Association Press, 1961), ch. V.
2. Dietrich Bonhoeffer, *No Rusty Swords: Letters, Lectures and Notes, 1928-1636*, ed. Edwin H. Robertson, trans. Edwin H. Robertson and John Bowden (New York and Evanston: Harper and Row, 1965), p. 20. See also Eberhard Bethge, *Dietrich Bonhoeffer: Theologian, Christian, Contemporary*, ed. Edwin H. Robertson, trans. E. Mosbacher et al. (London: Collins, 1970), esp. pp. 361-363; Clyde E. Fant, *Bonhoeffer: Worldly Preaching* (New York and Nashville: Thomas Nelson Inc., 1975), p. 140.
3. See C. K. Barrett, *The Holy Spirit and the Gospel Tradition* (London: S.P.C.K., 1954).

has preserved for us our Lord's own description of His direction and authority: "The Spirit of the Lord is upon me, because he has anointed me to preach..." (Luke 4:18). This characterization, quoted by Jesus from Isaiah 61:1-2, stands as something more than a comprehensive statement about His messianic uniqueness. It points out a requisite for the task of preaching. It reminds us that those who are sent to preach are first accredited for this service by the Holy Spirit. Peter understood this and referred once to "those who preached the good news to you through the Holy Spirit sent from heaven..." (I Peter 1:12). This requisite of being "anointed to preach" is highlighted throughout the Acts of the Apostles, where we see a succession of witnesses at work spreading the Christian message, all of them qualified because they were possessed and anointed by God's Spirit. As for the Book of Acts, F. F. Bruce has stated, "In all the book there is nothing which is unrelated to the Holy Spirit."[4] Christian sermons have no independent integrity or power; they find life and effectiveness only under the creative touch of God. The New Testament sums up this fundamental, inclusive, and compelling gift in the descriptive words *charisma* and *chrisma*.[5]

I

The concept of charismatic or anointed service reflects at least six distinct features which we experience through grace: (1) a sense of assertiveness by which to act; (2) a sense of being identified with divine will; (3) a perceived intensity because what is done relates to the highest frame of reference; (4) a sense of self-transcendence; (5) a kind of instinct for what is done; and (6) a knowledge that the deed is avowedly moral and religious in nature and reason, which is to say that the deed is traceable to God's prompting and power, and that it happens for His own reasons.

The word *charisma* is in common and widespread use in our

4. F. F. Bruce, *The Acts of the Apostles: The Greek Text with Introduction and Commentary* (Grand Rapids: Wm. B. Eerdmans Publishing Co., 1952), p. 30.
5. See *charisma*, by Hans Conzelman, and *chrisma*, by Walter Grundmann, *Theological Dictionary of the New Testament*, ed. Gerhard Friedrich, trans. Geoffrey W. Bromiley (Grand Rapids: Wm. B. Eerdmans Publishing Co., 1974), vol. IX, pp. 402-406, and 572, respectively.

time, and it is even being used in quite secular references and connections. Students of sociology are familiar with the way Max Weber (1864-1920) analyzed and applied the concept of charisma in relation to socio-political causes and structures.[6] As one of the pioneers in advancing the subject and concerns of the sociology of religion Weber worked in seriousness to trace the effects of religious beliefs within the wider social order. Weber commented extensively about the "charismatic figure" and his relation to the secular and spiritual order and institutions, seeing such a person as an agent in the process of breakthrough and morally ordered change. According to Weber's definition, "The term 'charisma' will be applied to a certain quality of an individual personality by virtue of which he is set apart from ordinary men and treated as endowed with supernatural, superhuman, or at least specifically exceptional powers or qualities."[7] The wideness of his definition enabled Weber to deal with the enlarged sphere of social life, but the distinctively religious connotations of his use of the term *charisma* cannot be missed. Max Weber wrote as a specialist in religious studies and not merely from the secular perspective of a sociologist. Although Weber kept the religious notion clearly focused as he did his work, some who followed him did not; and in widening the term to apply to heroism, populism, social movements, and behavioral control techniques, they secularized the meaning of *charisma* and identified it with the notion of special leadership per se. A clear example of this kind of application appeared some years ago in a Daedalus Library book entitled *Philosophers and Kings: Studies in Leadership.*[8] Recently John Howard Schutz has discussed the problem of how that originally religious term has been secularized and its meaning widened to the point of abuse.[9]

The fact is that the concept of charisma relates us centrally to the moral and spiritual order. Although there are some features

6. See *Max Weber on Charisma and Institution Building,* ed. S. N. Eisenstadt (Chicago: University of Chicago Press, 1968). See also Max Weber, *The Sociology of Religion,* ed. and trans. Ephraim Fischoff (Boston: Beacon Press, 1963), esp. pp. 2-3, 46-47.
7. *Max Weber on Charisma and Institution Building,* p. 48.
8. *Philosophers and Kings: Studies in Leadership,* ed. Dankwart A. Rustow (New York: George Braziller, 1970), esp. pp. 1-32 and 69-94.
9. See John Howard Schutz, "Charisma and Social Reality in Primitive Christianity," *The Journal of Religion,* vol. 54, no. 1 (January 1974).

that are common to both religious and social leadership roles—
projection, interplay between self and group, rapport, courageous
action, aggressiveness, and authority, to name but a few, there are
vast differences between the two. There are differences of values,
goals, source and use of power, and the spirit of the persons involved. There is a vast difference between being an instrumental
agent due to social demand and being an instrumental agent due
to sacred anointing.

Our emphasis here is on the sermon as a charismatic instrument in the will of God. We are dealing with a guided and girded
action called preaching, a happening in which nature and grace
make claim upon each other to effect an end through speech that
neither rhetorical nor sociological theory can fully explain. Anointing is integral to the very purpose of the sermon.

Understood as a way of orienting hearers to an experience with
God through truth, the sermon must open to the hearer's perception that which is on a transcendent level. The sermon must be
anointed to bear the needed noetic quality, bestow authoritative
knowledge, generate an awareness of awe, and help the hearer to
perceive the religious dimension as an immediately real order.[10]

Paul was so mindful of this decisive mission of preaching that
he wrote exultingly about the grace given to him to preach. Paul
declared that he was called "to make all men *see* . . ." (Eph. 3:9a).
In using *photisai* here, Paul reveals something beyond the ordinary,
meaning that in preaching he was concerned to go beyond mere
informing or announcing. Paul preached to illuminate men,[11]
heighten their level of consciousness, and grant contact with the
transcendent. Such results demand the participating presence of
God through His Spirit.

II

It must be said, then, that charisma in preaching has to do

---

10. For further insight into these categories, see Ralph W. Hood, Jr., "Religious Orientation and Experience of the Transcendent," *Journal for the
Scientific Study of Religion*, vol. 12, no. 4 (December 1973), pp. 441-448.
11. S. F. D. Salmond has commented, "The verb photisai is more than didaxai
or keruxai. It means to illuminate": *The Expositor's Greek Testament*, ed.
W. Robertson Nicoll (Grand Rapids: Wm. B. Eerdmans Publishing Co., n.d.),
vol. III, p. 307.

with the God-given ability to project an awareness of God in connection with the presentation of Biblical truth. Anointed preaching can effect a situation of "discernment-commitment," to use Ian T. Ramsey's phrase.[12] The sermon is an agency for "entailment." *Entailment* is the right word for what happens under anointed preaching because the fundamental end of the sermon is to guide the hearer in matching and fitting the Word of God to his life, indeed to ready him for living on God's terms.[13] The anointed preacher is an agent of mediated meaning, on the one hand, and mediated presence, on the other. It is this that makes the sermon more than mere speech.

1. Anointed preaching therefore carries the hearer beyond the limited benefits of the preacher's personality and rhetorical abilities. Anointing from God makes the preacher an agent of grace, a man furnished to point beyond himself—and to allow the beyondness of God to break through with immediacy and authority in his words. One aspect of that beyondness is the real awe of being confronted. It is an awe that is fear, but more than fear. It is a fascination, yet more than that.[14] It is an awareness of being before God, challenged, called to account, claimed. It is a sense of *kairos,* a special moment that is unique and individual.

2. Such preaching also involves something more than enthusiasm, as popularly understood.

Enthusiasm has meant many things to many people, and the term has been used in connection with both worthy and unworthy experiences. Enthusiasm has been linked with celestial inspiration, poetic fervor, fancied inspiration, ardent feeling, ill-regulated feeling, irrational agitation and movement, ardent zeal, emotionalism, etc.,[15] some of these states being too passionate to be rational and

---

12. See Ian T. Ramsey, *Religious Language* (New York: Macmillan Company, 1963), esp. pp. 11-54.
13. I have borrowed the term *entailment* from J. L. Austin, who used it to explain the refinement we give to words in expanding their meanings, in adjusting them to fit new and different objects. See Mats Furberg, *Saying and Meaning: A Main Theme in J. L. Austin's Philosophy* (Totana, N.J.: Rowman and Littlefield, 1971), esp. pp. 70-71, 166-167.
14. On this, see Rudolf Otto, *The Idea of the Holy,* ed. and trans. John W. Harvey, second edition (London: Oxford University Press, 1950), esp. pp. 8-40.
15. On the varied history it has had as a word, see Susie I. Tucker, *Enthusiasm: A Study in Semantic Change* (Cambridge: At the University Press, 1972).

too individual to be trusted. Charisma in preaching has nothing to do with what is dark and ambiguous, however passionate and lively. Charisma has to do with mediated meaning and mediated presence, with both affective and intellectual levels of life being addressed. Preaching involves speech, and speech must convey and bestow meaning. Preaching is not divorced from feelings or emotions but it is not directed primarily to them. Preaching at its best will have aliveness, interest, and excitement, but the plus element that makes it creative and convicting comes through neither the preacher's personal intensity nor the listener's rapt involvement but through the participant presence of God. It is true for the preacher today as for Zerubbabel of old, to whom the words were first directed, "Not by might, nor by power, but by my Spirit, says the Lord of hosts" (Zech. 4:6b).

3. Nor should charisma be confused with communalism, which is but a sense of contagious engagement between preacher and people.

Hailing as I do from the Black Church tradition in which a sense of community has helped to shape "black preaching," as it is called, I understand quite well the rich benefits for worship when preacher and congregation have achieved a sense of basic togetherness. This sense of communalism is a must particularly for the pastoral preaching task. But charisma in preaching carries the total group beyond mere social unity generated by common concern under the guidance of a common leader. Charisma conditions pastoral judgment and sharpens prophetic thrust. Charisma heightens the awareness level to a sense of participation with God, thus deepening the drama of worship. Here again we see meaning and presence working together. It must always be so, because as Jesus explained it, "God is spirit, and those who worship him must worship in spirit and truth" (John 4:24). Spirit and word— presence and meaning: it is to these that charisma keeps both preacher and people linked.

Dr. Henry H. Mitchell has called attention recently to the relation in the Black Church tradition between the Biblical concept of anointing and the common notion from ancient Africa of being possessed by deity.[16] In both traditions of belief there is a kind

---

16. Henry H. Mitchell, *Black Belief: Folk Beliefs of Blacks in America and West Africa* (New York and Evanston: Harper and Row, 1975), esp. pp. 136-152.

of claiming that is perceived. The claimed person is aware of a heightened purpose in what he does, while the people observe and acknowledge what happens to and through him. This tradition of possession carries the notion of being under divine influence, overwhelmed perhaps, but definitely being used by a higher order of meaning.

Black Church tradition carries the concern for possession by deity one step further in expecting the claim upon the preacher to become a claim upon those who hear and accept his message. In Black Church life, then, the preacher becomes the agent of contact with divine will and holy word. The preacher is understood to be a charismatic figure, and so is followed. It is this aspect of the Black Church tradition that accounts for the preacher's authority in the midst of his people, and that authoritative leadership is never greater than when the black preacher is guiding his people in a worship setting and speaking the Word from God. And since blacks consider worship as the most fundamental experience and expression of the self and the community, the preacher is free in his sermon to deal with any and every aspect of life (birth, death, politics, economics, social relations, etc.) because he is expected to bring "a word from the Lord" about the living of life. The radicalism of black preaching is rooted in this freedom, and this freedom is grounded on the authority of the preacher as a possessed and claimed man.

Given this tradition of belief within which to live and work, a tradition almost parallel to that of the Biblical prophetic order, the black preacher has usually given himself to his preaching task with such abandon that a heritage of freedom and involvement continues to characterize Black Church worship. This worship freedom is not purely Christian in origin—related as it is to an ancient African belief in being possessed by the deity, but it does carry us right to the heart of why the spoken word is so vital in Black Church worship. It also explains why certain forms of body action are allowed and sometimes encouraged in that worship setting. The charisma needed for preaching relates to all this, but sometimes it is also required as a prophetic check on excesses. Anointing is needed not only by preachers who seek freedom to speak effectively in settings that are more formal and sometimes closed to spontaneity; it is needed as well to provide balance in settings that are otherwise open and free. In all instances of preaching there

is the perennial need for anointing from God. Whatever the setting, whatever the worship style, whatever the background and
prevailing concepts within the respective group, there is need for
mediated meaning and mediated presence. The meaning does not
always diminish or dim our background and concepts, but the presence helps us to sift them, understand them, accept and adapt them,
and to use them fruitfully without prejudice or pride. This means
that ultimately we will not unwisely associate God with only one
worship style, nor will we mistakenly associate Him with only one
people.

III

This next word is about the obvious—but it must be said: charisma fulfills itself only in relation to persons.

Anointing is to benefit community. It is fulfilled and seen at its
effective best in relation to persons. Paul was underscoring this
when he commented, "To each is given the manifestation of the
Spirit for the common good" (I Cor. 12:7). Sermons must be prepared and preached with hearers in mind, and to be an effective
agent of meaning and presence each sermon must bear the form
and flavor of the personal.

The form and flavor of the personal is certainly evident when
the preacher is known to be a man identified with God, a committed believer and faithful servant of the Word. Charisma attends
those who have identified themselves with God and His will. The
man identified with the will of God is not afraid to be himself
or to use his gifts in God's honor. His experience of charisma en-
ables him to be active, assured, individuated, and assertive.

Long ago Thomas Carlyle argued eloquently for "an original
man; not a secondhand, borrowing or begging man." He continued
his comment, advising, "Let us stand on our own basis, at any
rate! On such shoes as we ourselves can get. On frost and mud,
if you will, but honestly on that;—on the reality and substance
which Nature gives *us*, not on the semblance, on the thing she has
given another than us!"[17]

Charismatic agents have always been able to stand on their

17. Thomas Carlyle, *On Heroes, Hero-Worship, and the Heroic in History,*
ed. Archibald MacMechan (Boston: Ginn and Co., 1901), p. 206.

own, use their own gifts, assert themselves with high warrant in a cause greater than their own lives. Willing to risk themselves under the influence of a great meaning, they become creative persons of social importance and characters of spiritual persuasion. They become integrative figures, leaders around whom men rally. Although a strong self-image and the ability to project oneself can be natural factors in the lives of some persons, charisma performs its indispensable ministry and accredits their identity in a still higher manner. Those who live unto God, fully committed, experience this, and those whom they serve can bear witness to it.

Respect for charisma has generated in some church circles an almost instinctive concern to preserve the good name and honor of the charismatic leader against even common criticisms. There are those anointed persons whose lives make others feel guilty of a kind of treason when their story is tampered with, or their faults isolated. Such individuated men, divinely gifted and committed, carry an atmosphere and become legendary. Carlyle once referred to "a few Poets who are accounted perfect; whom it were a kind of treason to find fault with."[18] Preachers with charisma are often "accounted perfect," but charisma must never be associated with faultlessness. Anointing from God is granted for specific services; it is not given to create legends nor to build a man beyond his true size.

Every preacher must watch the contagion that he generates and he must watch the basis on which that contagion grows. He must remain alert and forever separate and distinguish between self and service, and most especially between his opinions and God's Word.

There are some obvious dangers to church life when a charismatic person does not keep these distinctions in view. For one thing, the opinions of the preacher can sometimes become mandates by the sheer forcefulness of his personal presence and the flavor of his personal appeal. Church history is filled with instances when men became enamored of the power of charisma, and the end result was that the personal form and flavor were distorted and the effects of their service misapplied. Charismatic figures can distort and thwart what is personal when their opinions bind and constrict beyond the guidance of the Word. As for their

18. Ibid., p. 93.

opinions, charisma cannot make them more than they are, namely beliefs held and voiced with confidence but not yet tested nor positively proved. Church life is always endangered when opinions associated with charismatic leaders are accepted as final and binding.

Sermons demand a surer foundation than personal opinion. The conclusions they voice must be Biblically based. The applications they urge must be demonstrable in the light of the wisdom of Scripture. Sermons must be grounded on more than personal preference and must be free from personal prejudices. They must go beyond the collective opinion of the group one serves. The forces at work in a given group can be even more dangerous and erroneous than those at work in a single mind and heart. The Christian pulpit must not capitulate to popular notions of morals and ethics, nor must it yield to stereotyped views on race and social relations. To yield a prophetic word in favor of acceptable and popular prejudices is but to allow a configuration of chaos. Personal opinion—even of the charismatic leader—is not always right, and public opinion—even of the Church in a given era—is not always wise.[19] Not only is charisma fulfilled in relation to persons, it is to be checked against Biblical principles. This keeps the charismatic agent right, relevant, and regulated.

The responsible preacher will have opinions, as will anyone who thinks, but he should check them against the Word before uttering them in a worship setting. The preacher will hear opinions, as will anyone who listens long to others, but he must assess them in the light of the Word. He will influence opinion, as will anyone in the social arena, but he should use the informing Word as he carries out his work. In this way the preacher can seek to guarantee that his appeal and authority serve more than the end of self-expression. He can thereby serve a purpose higher than himself— and larger than the group which looks to him as leader.

IV

Given the purpose of anointing from God, namely to make the preacher an agent of mediated meaning and presence, it must

19. See Martin E. Marty, *The Improper Opinion: Mass Media and the Christian Faith* (Philadelphia: Westminster Press, 1961), esp. pp. 65ff.

be clearly understood that the charismatic thrust of the sermon is first evident in the sermon idea or insight. Preaching mediates meaning from the Word of God. Sermon charisma is granted to serve Biblical meanings applied to human needs.

The chief end of a sermon is to make an informed, aroused, and God-committed person. Central to this end is the hearer's awareness of God in connection with a basic Biblical insight addressed to his listening level and state of life. The shaping of such a sermon constitutes the preacher's undertaking, but the spirit and substance of that sermon must be rooted in God if understanding and insight are to be effected. Insight is the crucial concern in planning the sermon, for as Bernard J. F. Lonergan has well stated, "Once one has understood, one has crossed a divide."[20] This is true for both preacher and hearer. Once the preacher has gained insight into the textual meaning and its application, he has crossed the divide and can use the text for a sermon; once the hearer has heard and seen the insight addressed to him, he has crossed the divide and is responsible to its claim on him.

It is sometimes overlooked that preaching is essentially oral for reasons of greater impact through insight. True hearing is meant to allow (and force) a kind of seeing. The very word *idea* —whether from the Greek *eidon* or *idea*, or from the Latin *video*— has to do with seeing, perceiving, or experiencing something.[21] Intent on communicating, the God-anointed preacher will work wisely with his words in seeking to mediate the insight from God's Word.

It is a well-known fact that we all tend to see more clearly when something is shown to us through striking speech, especially when the words heard are pictorial in suggestion. The sound itself becomes an inward event, and the meaning stands as part of the hearer's experience. The very act of preaching brings truth within the range of a hearer in order that he may see, understand, be aroused, and act. The words of the sermon must be planned to express and share Biblical insight. Rooted as it is in God's Word,

20. Bernard J. F. Longeran, *Insight: A Study of Human Understanding* (New York: Philosophical Library, 1956), p. 6.
21. On the Greek terms see Wilhelm Michaelis's article in *Theological Dictionary of the New Testament*, ed. Gerhard Friedrich, trans. Geoffrey W. Bromiley (Grand Rapids: Wm. B. Eerdmans Publishing Co., 1967), vol. V, pp. 315-343.

the insight will bear the signature of divine presence. It will also effect a definite psychic flow within the hearer that is spiritual in origin and purpose.

This kind of result is due, in part, to the very psychology of language itself. Quite beyond the meanings that words suggest and convey, language affects consciousness itself. Preaching relates speaker and hearer in a lively context where concepts, consciousness, and claim all go together. We all hear words that carry meanings which move us from the state of mere awareness to attitudes out of which action of some kind follows. Consciousness and meaning follow from hearing, but there is a deeper demand on us when a sense of claim is realized upon our being addressed. It is at this point that the effects of charisma in preaching become imperative. The self needs more than meanings to be fully aroused; the self also needs a sense of divine presence. The charisma that attends preaching not only declares meanings, it illuminates and conveys a sense of claim. This aspect of preaching is a direct result of the participating presence of God through His Spirit. The Holy Spirit blesses the hearing occasion with effects far beyond the normal range of the psychology of language. Anointed preaching is always more than mere speech. It bears a realization of engagement with God.

It is important that preaching be anointed because the sermons we create are always less than the texts we use. The preparation and delivery of sermons always involve an inherent difficulty. That difficulty is: how to break through the limitations of what is only human. That difficulty is overcome by appeal to a higher order. The answer is charisma, anointing from God. In the delivery of a sermon we must deal with the problem that what is being heard—and what is yet to be heard—is not there all at once. This means that attention and patient listening are demanded. There must be something more at work than just a sense of logical flow to encourage interest in continued listening. With the delivery of every sermon we must deal with the "biology of time."[22] The sermon is never a whole thing as we are giving it; we give only a part at a time. This means that the hearing moment is so precarious that something more is needed for preaching besides words. Charisma

22. This expression has been used with reference to hearing music. See David Burrows, "Music and the Biology of Time," *Perspectives of New Music* (Fall-Winter 1972), Tenth Anniversary Issue, pp. 241-249.

solves this problem by granting a sense of presence and by quickening within the hearer a sense of promise of mediated meaning from the whole. The whole is important because the spoken sermon is only part of the process. It is not a complete thing by itself; it is an agency of meaning and presence.

Both listener and preacher undergo the experience of the sermon: the preacher as shaper of the words and style, the listener as the one alerted by its signals of meaning. Both preacher and listener share in the meaning and the presence. Both share in the vision of truth, and when both respect its message and accept its thrust, the time of hearing is experienced as reliable, qualitative, revelational, and integral.

Helmut Thielicke, whose superlative preaching holds a flame by which many preachers have sat to warm themselves, has confessed his own deep admiration for the sermons of Charles Haddon Spurgeon (1834-1892). In fact, Thielicke has advised every preacher concerned about better preaching to study Spurgeon's preaching "to learn what a sermon can be and what it can give."[23] His advice came after a prolonged and fruitful "encounter with Spurgeon," as he called it, meaning a time of studying and sifting Spurgeon's exemplary sermons, together with his thoughtful lectures to his students on the art of preaching. Thielicke assessed Spurgeon's sermons as charismatic, the work of a man who had the "gift of charismatic hearing."[24] He meant by this that Spurgeon first lingered in the presence of God to hear Him speak before moving forth to say anything on God's behalf. Spurgeon's sermons *are* charismatic; even in written form they evidence a powerful claim that makes us hear. Spurgeon's secret of pulpit power was not his ready wit, nor his exuberant eloquence, but his anointing. The glow is still left from his ministry, and one senses it afresh as his sermons are reviewed.[25] Though dead, he still speaks because he had the rich anointing of the Higher Voice.

Jane Steger, on one of the last pages of her illuminating book *Leaves from a Secret Journal,* tells of the "awestruck emotion" she

---

23. Helmut Thielicke, *Encounter with Spurgeon*, trans. John W. Doberstein (Philadelphia: Fortress Press, 1963), p. 3.
24. Ibid.
25. See *Sermons of Rev. C. H. Spurgeon of London*, 20 vols. (New York: Funk and Wagnalls Co., 1857). See also *Great Pulpit Masters* (New York: Fleming H. Revell Co., 1949), vol II, *Charles H. Spurgeon*, esp. the sermon "Songs in the Night," pp. 211-235.

experienced when as a girl of eleven years of age she would somtimes retire to a spare bedroom of the house and pull out a certain bureau drawer in which "a certain picture of Him, a photograph of an Ecce Homo by one of the old masters" was kept. That was always a time of deep excitement for her.

> What it did to me I never knew exactly—only the deep secret of the picture touched the deepest in me, moving me with inexpressible awe and devotion, sifting me down and down into the depths of my being. That great Personality spoke to my child self in a language so deep that I do not know even now quite how to interpret it. The emotion that He evoked in the little girl of eleven, He evokes in me now; . . . I am, and always shall be, the unutterably grateful, humble, and adoring follower of the Lord Jesus Christ.[26]

Here is the secret of power in Christian witness, for preacher and people: Jesus "that great Personality" continues with us in word and presence. He companions, leads and speaks to us, always evoking emotion that spills over in praise and proclamation.

True preaching is the sharing of His words and the mediation of His presence, through the anointing of His indwelling Spirit. The New Testament word for this ability and action is *charisma*.

---

26. Jane Steger, *Leaves from a Secret Journal* (Boston: Little, Brown and Company, 1926), p. 153.

INDEX

115